T0194845

Five
Smooth Stones
WHAT I KNOW ABOUT GOD, FOR SURE

Larry LaDell Robertson

authorHOUSE®

AuthorHouse™
1663 Liberty Drive
Bloomington, IN 47403
www.authorhouse.com
Phone: 1 (800) 839-8640

Published by AuthorHouse 10/29/2019

ISBN: 978-1-7283-3303-8 (sc)
ISBN: 978-1-7283-3301-4 (hc)
ISBN: 978-1-7283-3302-1 (e)

Library of Congress Control Number: 2019916921

Print information available on the last page.

CONTENTS

DEDICATION

This book is dedicated to my help-meet, cheerleader, soulmate, and best friend, my lovely and supportive wife, Ramona. It's through my relationship with you that I know how it truly feels to be loved, supported and encouraged. I hope I've made you proud. And to my daughters, Jesseca and Jazzmin, thank you for your undeniable encouragement and inspiration.

I also dedicate this work to some remarkable spiritual leaders, teachers, and advisors (past and present) who have influenced my journey to greater awareness and illumination. Audience with you helped me realize and recognize the Father's teachings and plans for me. Reaching me was a part of your Divine assignment.

I thank God for you all.

INTRODUCTION

A Relationship with God

This past January, I celebrated 54 years of life. I was pleasantly surprised but proud when I realized that each one of those years was spent as a member of a church. Be it large, mid-sized or small, traditional, progressive, or esoteric, I made good on my promise to myself to always be connected and affiliated with a body of like believers, working out our soul salvation, together. As such, I've listened to priests, prophets, and preachers impart their interpretation of scripture and what "thus saith the Lord." Some made me laugh, some made me cry. Some yelled and screamed while other were more academic, articulate and soft-spoken. Others made me think in new ways while some were downright insulting and made me angry. I don't remember them all but the ones I do remember were meant for me to hear.

One of the best sermons I've heard was delivered by my childhood and very first pastor, the late Reverend Doctor John L. Conner. It was entitled "a relationship with God." If I close my eyes and still myself, I can see this tall, caramel-hued man with a commanding presence and a booming voice, pointing to members of the congregation as if he was speaking to them individually, posing what I now consider an important and life-changing question: do you have a relationship with God? I was a junior in high school, so I wasn't surprised when my answer to the question was no, I did not have a relationship with God. I knew of God. I believed in God. Rev. Conner even baptized me in the name of the Father, Son and Holy Spirit: all that God Is. And I was sure to be offended and even turned-up my nose to people who were silly enough not believe in God. But no, I didn't and really didn't understand what it meant. I believe this is when my true soul journey began.

According to Dr. Conner, when you have a relationship with God you:
1. Depend on Him for guidance and protection (rather than man) and so there's nothing to fear;
2. Know that He hears you when you speak, and you hear Him when He speaks; and
3. Are confident that He goes before you and makes a way, sometimes when there seems to be no way.

In essence, to have a relationship with God means that you know without trepidation, hesitation, or (as the old Christians say) beyond a shadow of doubt that God wants you to live a life without worry, without sickness, and without lack. You solemnly believe that God's will for you is complete and sustained favor and success.

So now, decades after that message, I can say yes, I have a unique and authentic relationship with God. And through this relationship, I've been able to experience life in an entirely different and a more fulfilling way than before. I'm not afraid of situations and people anymore. I don't worry about conditions or circumstances anymore. I don't expect or accept lack and limitation on any level; not anymore. Through my relationship with God, I've learned that His will for me is absolute good and I renounce, reject, and cancel all thoughts, opinions, and teachings to the contrary. Suffering, sickness, and lack are not good things, so I deem it ridiculous to think that these things are God's will for me.

I received the assignment to write this book from God with the purpose of compelling believers and non-believers to develop a relationship with God. I've been so enlightened and blessed through this journey that I can't imagine how my life would look right now absent my relationship with God. I said to God, Father, I can't do this. What will people say? I'm not an ordained minister, prophet, or seer. I don't have a degree in theology and not a big fan of "my way or the highway" books. You know those books that make you out to be intellectually challenged if you disagreed with what it posits. Besides a few friends and my family, who's going to buy and read it? I'm just a regular hard-working guy with a passion for writing and a dream of being an author, willing to share what I know about God for sure. That's when He said, "tell them about me, and only what you know for sure. Your goal isn't to sell books. It's to challenge mindsets and impart what you've come to know as the truth. Get the message out and I'll do the rest." So, in these 51,000 plus words, I present my truth, what's working, and what I've come to know about God and myself, for sure.

This is an awesome assignment and I pray that the information I share will give you energy and curiosity to work on your relationship with the Father. And as you create your plan and do the work, I pray that your life is enhanced in big, bold, and beautiful ways. This work should in no way be confused with a scholarly theological research project or a religious dissertation of any kind. God and I wrote this book with reliance on my experiences, truths I've come to know, conversations with others, and multiple versions of the Holy Bible. There is an over-arching and compelling message of empowerment and new thinking presented in this work and because it's based on my personal experiences and my interpretations of selected scripture, I don't feel a need to over-validate or prove a thing. I am simply sharing what I've learned and have come to know for sure, in a big, bold, and life-changing way.

In the spirit of learning and understanding, I invite you to roll up the sleeves of your mind and enjoy these lessons and (hopefully) discoveries. Remember, to discover means to realize something that already exists. My pray is that you discover some inspiring and powerful things about God and yourself that, when you really think about it, have been inside of you and around you all along.

At the end of each chapter, you will find a section tagged "think on these things." In these sections, I pose questions to help you realize and understand your discoveries and kick-start your spiritual work, should you choose action over complacency in this regard. Use it personally in your meditation, reflection and study or use it in discussions with your family, friends, and bible study groups. The goal is not to persuade. The goal is to illuminate. If you only walk away with one lesson, one idea, or one area of your spiritual self that you want to change, the purpose of this work has been fulfilled.

CHAPTER 1

The Truth Shall Make You Free

• • ● • •

When given the assignment to write this book, I was also given the title: Five Smooth Stones. Knowing that it had a biblical or religious reference, I did some research, which took me to the popular and positive story of David and Goliath. The story is found in First Samuel 17: 1-53. This scripture serves as the foundational reference for this book. Here is the story as depicted by the author of First Samuel, believed by some to be Samuel himself. I've chosen the New International Version (NIV) of the story for clarity and understanding.

1 Samuel 17:1-53 New International Version (NIV)

(17:1) Now the Philistines gathered their forces for war and assembled in Sokoh in Judah. They pitched camp at Ephes Damminm, between Sokoh and Azekah. (2) Saul and the Israelites assembled and camped in the Valley of Elah and drew up their battle line to meet the Philistines. (3) The Philistines occupied one hill and the Israelites another, with the valley between them. (4) A champion named Goliath, who was from Gath, came out of the Philistine camp. His height was six cubits and a span (about 9 feet and 9 inches). (5) He had a bronze helmet on his head and wore a coat of scale armor of bronze weighing five thousand shekels (about 125 pounds) (6) on his legs he wore bronze greaves, and a bronze javelin was slung on his back. (7) His spear shaft was like a weaver's rod, and its iron point weighed six hundred shekels (about 15 pounds). His shield bearer went ahead of him.

(8) Goliath stood and shouted to the ranks of Israel, "Why do you come out and line up for battle? Am I not a Philistine, and are you not the servants of Saul? Choose a man and have him come down to me. (9) If he is able to fight and kill me, we will become your subjects; but if I overcome him and kill him, you will become our subjects and serve us." (10) Then the Philistine said, "This day I defy the armies of Israel. Give me a man and let us fight each other." (11) On hearing the Philistine's words, Saul and all the Israelites were dismayed and terrified. (12) Now David was the son of an Ephrathite named Jesse, who was from Bethlehem in Judah. Jesse had eight sons and in Saul's time he was very old. (13) Jesse's three oldest sons had followed Saul to the war: The firstborn was Eliab; the second Abinadab; and the third, Shammah. (14) David was the youngest. The three oldest followed Saul, (15) but David went back and forth from Saul to tend his father's sheep at Bethlehem.

(16) For forty days the Philistine came forward every morning and evening and took his stand. (17) Now Jesse said to his son David, "Take the ephah of roasted grain and these ten loaves of bread for your brothers and hurry to their camp. (18) Take along these ten cheeses to the commander of their unit. See how your brothers are and bring back some assurance from them. (19) They are with Saul and all the men of Israel in the Valley of Elah, fighting against the Philistines."

(20) Early in the morning David left the flock in the care of a shepherd, loaded up and set out, as Jesse had directed. He reached the camp as the army was going

out to its battle positions, shouting the war cry. (21) Israel and the Philistines were drawing up their lines facing each other. (22) David left his things with the keeper of supplies, ran to the battle lines and asked his brothers how they were. (23) As he was talking with them, Goliath, the Philistine champion from Gath, stepped out from his lines and shouted his usual defiance, and David heard it. (24) Whenever the Israelites saw the man, they all fled from him in great fear.

(25) Now the Israelites had been saying, "Do you see how this man keeps coming out? He comes out to defy Israel. The king will give great wealth to the man who kills him. He will also give him his daughter in marriage and will exempt his family from taxes in Israel." (26) David asked the men standing near him, "What will be done for the man who kills this Philistine and removes this disgrace from Israel? Who is this uncircumcised Philistine that he should defy the armies of the living God? (27) They repeated to him what they had been saying and told him, "This is what will be done for the man who kills him."

(28) When Eliab, David's oldest brother, heard him speaking with the men, he burned with anger at him and asked, "Why have you come down here? And with whom did you leave those few sheep in the wilderness? I know how conceited you are and how wicked your heart is; you came down only to watch the battle."

(29) "Now what have I done?" said David. "Can't I even speak?" (30) He then turned away to someone else and brought up the same matter, and the men answered him as before. (31) What David said was overheard and reported to Saul, and Saul sent for him. (32) David said to Saul, "Let no one lose heart on account of this Philistine; your servant will go and fight him." (33) Saul replied, "You are not able to go out against this Philistine and

fight him; you are only a young man, and he has been a warrior from his youth."

(34) But David said to Saul, "Your servant has been keeping his father's sheep. When a lion or a bear came and carried off a sheep from the flock, (35) I went after it, struck it and rescued the sheep from its mouth. When it turned on me, I seized it by its hair, struck it and killed it. (36) Your servant has killed both the lion and the bear; this uncircumcised Philistine will be like one of them because he has defied the armies of the living God. (37) The Lord who rescued me from the paw of the lion and the paw of the bear will rescue me from the hand of the Philistine." Saul said to David, "Go, and the Lord be with you."

(38) Then Saul dressed David in his own tunic. He put a coat of armor on him and a bronze helmet on his head. (39) David fastened on his sword over the tunic and tried walking around, because he was not used to them. "I cannot go in the these," he said to Saul, "because I am not used to them." So, he took them off. (40) Then he took his staff in his hand, chose **five smooth stones** from the stream, put them in the pouch of his shepherd's bag and, with his sling in his hand, approached the Philistine.

(41) Meanwhile, the Philistine, with his shield bearer in front of him, kept coming closer to David. (42) He looked David over and saw that he was a little more than a boy, glowing with health and handsome, and he despised him. (43) He said to David, "Am I a dog, that you come at me with sticks? And the Philistine cursed David by his gods. (44) "Come here," he said, "and I'll give your flesh to the birds and the wild animals."

(45) David said to the Philistine, "You come against me with sword and spear and javelin, but I come against you in the name of the Lord Almighty, the God of the armies of Israel, whom you have defied. (46) This day

the Lord will deliver you into my hands and I'll strike you down and cut off your head. This very day I will give the carcasses of the Philistine army to the birds and the wild animals, and the whole world will know that it is not by sword or spear that the Lord sees; for the battle is the Lord's, and he will give all of you into our hands."

(48) As the Philistine moved closer to attack him, David ran quickly toward the battle line to meet him. (49) Reaching into his bag and taking out a stone, he slung it and struck the Philistine on the forehead. The stone sank into his forehead, and he fell face down on the ground. (50) So, David triumphed over the Philistine with a sling and a stone; without a sword in his hand he struck down the Philistine and killed him. (51) David ran and stood over him. He took hold of the Philistine's sword and drew it from the sheath. After he killed him, he cut off his head with the sword. When the Philistines saw that their hero was dead, they turned and ran.

This story of David's victory over Goliath and the Philistines is one of the most popular and referenced "triumph over adversity" stories of the bible. To the casual reader, it's a story about succeeding against the odds, but to the spiritual truth student (whoever comes to learn) the potency of this account draws your attention from what appears as impossible to conquer (Goliath) to the possible, which is the magnificence and power of God (David). The story is the focal reference of this book because it supports the concept of spiritual freedom.

I define Spiritual freedom as a state of mind where (even when faced with the most dire evidence) there is an assurance of deliverance, success, and victory. My mind is impenetrable to even the illusion of being fearful or attacked by any giant or foe and there is no possibility of failure or defeat. When David accepted the assignment by God to defeat Goliath, the scripture says he chose five smooth stones, put them in his pouch and approached the Philistine. He didn't run from the bully, the giant, the evil hero. In his freedom, he ran <u>toward</u> Goliath. In his mind and in actions, there was no hint of the possibility of failure. He was not afraid because fear is a form of bondage. He was not embarrassed, nor did he feel inadequate because inferiority and low self-esteem are forms of bondage. He did not waiver and did not second guess what he heard from God. Doubt of any kind is a form of bondage. Nor did he feel ill-equipped or unprepared as lack is a form of bondage. Freedom, particularly spiritual freedom, and bondage cannot exist in the same space. With confidence and assurance, he expressed his spiritual freedom and boldly prophesied to the giant, "this day, the Lord will deliver you into my hands and I'll strike you down and cut off your head and give your carcasses to the birds and wild animals, and the world will know that there is a God in Israel."

In the human realm of our experiences, we are forced to consider the facts that present themselves in all situations, even those that are less than optimal. These facts can also come disguised as truths. When I was a smoker, I was aware of the fact that smoking cigarettes made me highly susceptible to lung cancer. When I was severely overweight, I was faced with the fact that obesity can lead to high blood pressure, diabetes, sleep apnea, and heart disease, just to name a few. My father battled prostate cancer when he was alive. I was faced with the fact that being an African-American male with a family history of prostate cancer, I am 30% more likely to acquire it than others.

In the David and Goliath story, David had to deal with some obvious and daunting facts himself:

- David was very young man; just a little more than a boy;
- Although he defended his flock and himself against lions and bears in the wild, he was not an experienced soldier;
- He was an errand boy for his family, delivering bread and cheese to his older brothers and others in the army;
- Where Goliath had armor, the only thing David had was a spear, some stones and a sling shot;
- Goliath was a nine-foot bully with a seemingly terrifying presence; and
- Goliath could kill David with one forceful blow.

But here is the good news: those who believe and have a cultivated relationship with God are not bound by the limitations of the facts in any situation. Within the spiritual realm of our being, there is freedom from the bondage of mere facts. Spiritually, the believer moves forward and runs toward the giant as David did, with power and in truth.

Truth is the awareness and confidence in the awareness that God's will for you is good and only good. Because He is our Father, God wants us to have life and not just "coming up on the rough side of the mountain" life but abundant life. His will for us is a life in a body without pain, sickness or disease. Truth is knowing that with Him every giant or Goliath can be defeated. Right here right now while you're reading these words, begin to reject that old "back woods" teaching you may have experienced; teachings that suggested that it's God's will for you to be sick or broke or unhappy. Teachings that suggested that God is punishing you for past mistakes and that you have to spend the rest of your life in perpetual repentance. Those are thoughts of restriction and bondage. I know for sure that God wants you, me, and all His children to be happy and free. It was in this truth that David was able to say to Goliath, "you come against me with sword and spear and javelin, but I come against you in the name of the Lord Almighty." In this truth and with this spiritual freedom, David triumphed over Goliath and the Philistine army retreated and many died.

Several year ago, a challenge presented itself in my body. Admittedly, I am a big baby when it comes to pain but what I experienced would have been labeled nearly unbearable by people with the highest tolerance for pain. My primary care physician at the time proved to be less than caring and overall ineffective in helping me out of my situation. He would say, "Larry, you've got to man-up. There are people who deal with pain three times greater than what you're dealing with." I won't share the exact words I used in response to his counsel, but I fired him and refused to be treated by him again. Through casual conversation with one of the nurses in the clinic, God sent me Dr. Michelle. She was technically a surgeon and only taking referral cases from other doctors in the clinic. Well after I cussed out and fired my primary care doctor, I just knew she wouldn't take my case. After God (I believe) spoke to her, she agreed to take me on as a new patient and without a referral.

When I first met her, I was pleased and relieved. She was very thorough, patient and smart. I thanked her for taking me on as a new patient without a referral and promised her a platter of my famous triple chocolate chip cookies if she "got me right." She laughed and commented that chocolate chip cookies were her favorite, so she had no choice but to "get me right," if only for the sweet treat.

She examined me and ran several tests to fully understand my condition. She said that she did not believe in pain, but she didn't support drug addiction either. She prescribed the highest potency non-narcotic pain medicine she could. Though the pain medication barely took the edge off, I counted this as a blessing and better than taking 16-18 over-the-counter naproxen pills every day, which I did for weeks. She also prescribed medication that is typically used for this condition, but it did not work. After a second battery of tests and exams, she had no clear plan to defeat this challenge. Suddenly, I (like David) was faced with a myriad of facts of my own to work through:

- Medications at their highest dosage typically used to treat and cure this challenge did not work in my body;
- The only medications available to combat the excruciating pain were opioids which would restrict my ability to drive, work, and engage in normal daily activities. These drugs also had side effects and a high probability of addiction, so these drugs were not the answer;
- Although Dr. Michelle was an experienced physician and surgeon, I stumped her, as she admitted she'd never seen a case like mine before; and
- If not treated and corrected, this condition would lead to other and more serious and chronic conditions, negatively impacting my quality of life.

During a subsequent appointment with Dr. Michelle, she suggested surgery but as an exploratory approach because she had no sure plan. Her thinking was if she could actually "go in" and see what was going on up close and personal, maybe a solution could come. Although she cautioned that the surgery could result in no solution, I agreed to the procedure. So, in the throes of all these facts, all I had was the truth:

- There is absolutely, positively nothing too hard for God to cure, fix, or solve;
- God's will for me is life and that more abundantly;
- Because of grace and mercy, I did not have to "earn" the gift of healing from my Father - it was my rite of passage;
- My past transgressions had been forgiven and were not the cause of this challenge in my body; and
- I can come against anything in the name of the Lord Almighty and be victorious, even this.

In post-op, Dr. Michelle said she did try something she'd never tried before but was not sure it was going to work. She instructed me to get rest, take a week off work, and begin taking the pain medication immediately as the next three days were going to be hell. And she wasn't lying. Those three days were extremely difficult, but on the fourth day, I felt better than I'd felt in months. Each day, I felt better and better.

I baked Dr. Michelle a platter (36) of my triple chocolate chip cookies and went to my scheduled one-week follow-up appointment. When the nurse called my name, I followed her to the examination room. Dr. Michelle and two of the nurses that I had befriended were waiting for me. The room turned quiet. All eyes fell on me. Dr. Michelle asked me, "on a scale of one to ten with ten being outstanding, how do you feel?" I replied, 15 and handed her the platter of cookies I had hidden behind my back. This woman of Jewish practice and faith began to jump up and down with excitement. In fact, all four of us were jumping, laughing, and thanking God in our own way. She conducted an exam and sent me to the lab for stat blood work to check on the condition of the condition. It was confirmed. Just as David defeated Goliath and the truth defeated the facts, I was healed. We chatted and ate cookies before she had to move on with her day. She said, "now be careful because this can reoccur." I responded, "nonsense! I'm free and plan on staying free. This is done!"

As John wrote in John 8:31-32 and 36 New King James Version (NKJV), "then said Jesus to those Jews which believed on Him, if ye continue in my word, then are ye my disciples indeed; And ye shall know the truth, and the truth shall make you free. If the Son therefore shall make you free, ye shall be free indeed." In this spiritual freedom, this truth, my truth, what I know for sure about God, I was made free.

I am careful and deliberate in using the words "made free." Some say, "set free," but in my experience to be set free sounds temporary and conditional. If something (or someone) sets you free, that thing or person can capture you again. To be made free is permanent. Once you've been made free, there is no going back. In this favor, you, me, we enjoy permanent relief from any unwanted circumstance, even the daunting facts or a nine-foot formidable giant.

In the 46th verse of our foundational reference, David said to Goliath, "I come against you in the name of the Lord Almighty." When "Goliaths" come against us in our experiences (i.e., worry, doubt, lack, marital problems, etc.) how do we, the believer come against these things? How do you practice and express your truth and spiritual freedom? I have learned to do this through affirmations.

I define an affirmation as a statement of truth that cancels, kills, or "cuts off the head" of thoughts of negativity and distress; thoughts that pull us away from truth-based living toward mere fact-based living. To affirm means to say something positively. It means to declare firmly and assert something to be true. Affirmations assert that what you want to be true is indeed true.

In science, a positive cancels a negative. In physics, light cancels darkness. In accounting, a credit is posted against a debit. On my spiritual journey, I know for certain that well-developed and firmly stated affirmations serve as a first and meaningful response that will "come against" these giant challenges that appear in our experiences.

You may ask, how do I word an affirmation? How are they developed? First and foremost, it's important not to make this a laborious chore. Creating these statements is not difficult at all. You don't have to be a theologian or English major to create these statements of truth and expectancy. An easy way to begin is by developing the practice of calling something that may not exist or may not be firm in consciousness into existence. Suppose you really believed that your words had power. Just as the Father did when He created the universe. Suppose whatever you called forth would show-up in your experience. Imagine how it would look, how you would feel, how different and better your circumstance would be. Those words (I like writing them down) become affirmations. Here are some personal examples:

- I am not what my adversary says I am. I am an intelligent child of God. No one can harm or disturb me.
- There is only peace, joy, happiness and love in my home. Nothing to the contrary can enter or dwell here.
- I am led by the Christ spirit within me. I am safe, fearless and protected.

And so it is! Similar to Amen, and so it is cements your words in consciousness and affirms that it's already done. Practice writing and speaking your personal affirmations. Your words will not return void. I know this for sure.

Think on These Things

1. How would you describe your current relationship with God? If you had to explain it to another person, how would you describe it?
2. Complete this sentence, I know for certain, God's will for me is
   _____!
3. What is spiritual freedom? Describe spiritual freedom through the foundational bible story.
4. What's the difference between a fact and the truth?
5. Develop three personal affirmations each week. Speak them daily. Journal your life experience as it begins to change.

CHAPTER 2

God Is Good

• ● ● ● •

"Do not conform to the patterns of this world but be transformed by the renewing of your mind. Then you will be able to test and approve what God's will is – His good pleasing and perfect will," (Romans 12:2 NIV).

As a child growing up in a traditional Baptist church, I was led to believe that God was a vengeful, jealous, and angry man, who sat high and looked low, watching the things I did, hearing the things I said, and reading all my thoughts. I was taught to fear Him and lead a life that would not agitate his wrath because He could "take me out" with the mere flaring of his nostrils. Yikes!

Conversely, as a member of the choir, I would stand and sing songs that boasted of the love and goodness of God; songs like His Yoke is Easy, He's Sweet I Know, and He's Been So Good. Always inquisitive and mature beyond my years, it was curious to me that God could be that complex, but what did I know? Maybe, like a parent, God was slow to punish and quick to care. And what was this book that everyone spoke about? God had this giant book, where He kept track of all the good things I did and the bad as well. And at some point, He was going to review my record and there had better be more good than bad, or I was (as the senior saints used to say) going to bust hell wide open. At the time, that's what I was supposed to believe and not question.

As I got older and even more inquisitive, this concept of a bi-polar God pressed on me more and more and needed to be resolved in my soul. I was having a hard time really understanding who and what God was. I don't remember the exact day or who the minister was who said it, but I heard a scripture that helped me tremendously. It was Romans 12:2. This was an enlightening and pivotal point in my spiritual journey. I pulled it apart, studied it and discovered some life-changing lessons.

1. **Do not conform to the patterns of this world** – I am an individual with my own thoughts, beliefs and disbeliefs. I do not owe an apology or explanation to anyone, relative to what I know and think about my God. I do not have to conform or think like everyone else, even if they are church people. Even if they are my elders, who I've respected and emulated since my childhood. Even if it does not align with the doctrine that I have been taught, I have the right, agency, and license to believe and serve God in a manner that's personal and meaningful to me and pleasing to Him.

2. **...But be ye transformed** – To be transformed means more than benign change. I define transformation as change that is so profound that your post transformational state is unrecognizable. If I dyed my hair red, most people would recognize me with the aid of a stare or double glance. But if I lost a considerable amount of weight, people may walk right past me as if I were a stranger because they didn't recognize me. Transformation means that you have given away so much of the old you that you are brand new. Transformation, in this regard, is positive. It speaks to the growth and the achievement of a spiritual milestone and demonstration.

3. **By the renewing** – Renewing here is not like renewing a membership to a professional association or renewing a subscription to a magazine. That renewal means continuation. Renewal in the spiritual realm means a higher level of engagement or conviction. After my cousin made her transition at the age of 11 from Leukemia in her body, I had a renewed conviction to support organizations that were committed to eradicating

childhood death from terminal illnesses. After visiting several historically Black colleges and universities, I had a renewed conviction to donate annually to the United Negro College Fund. Once I reconciled what I believed about God, I did not retreat and keep my transformation dormant. I was excited about expressing my thoughts about God in this new way.

4.   **...Of your mind** – God is so awesome. He gave me the choice of how to believe in Him and express my belief without fear or trepidation. I get to serve God according to my belief, what I believe in my mind. I get to control my mind and not conform to the ways of others (as popular as their views and thinking may be). I control my mind, therefore I control my experience. Some people are upset, concerned and even afraid because of the outcome of the last presidential election. People have inflicted restrictions on their spending and travel because of the man who sits in the White House. These people (on the job, at the barbershop and in the church) are quick to advise and counsel others to live in fear of this modern-day Philistine. But I am not afraid. I will not place restrictions on this abundant life I've been given to live. The earth belongs to God and I go free. Sounds like an affirmation to me!

5.   **Then you will be able to test and approve what God's will is – His good, pleasing and perfect will** – Only through a renewed mind and transformation are you able to testify to the goodness of God. Until you ramp up your conviction and understanding about a will for you that is pleasing, good and perfect, you can never be transformed and can never grow or live the abundant life that God wants you to live. Believing the same old thing and doing the same old thing will always yield the same old results. In the bible, the disciples had been fishing all night and had not caught one fish. Jesus told them to drop their nets on the right side. They caught so many fish, they could hardly pull the full nets onto the boat. I drop my spiritual net on the other side and receive all the good God has in store for me, first in my mind.

When you've been transformed to understand that God is good and His will for you is all things good, pleasing and perfect, you look at the world differently. Things once deemed impossible become possible. You begin to defy the facts and anchor your trust in truth. In this mindset of spiritual freedom, you hear, see, smell, taste and touch things differently. You have a reaction (sometimes physically) to traditions, rituals, and practices that are counter to your renewed understanding. You simply cannot tolerate them anymore. That's a good sign. It means that you have lifted your net from the left and lowered it on the right. You no longer want to lower it on the left. You've been successful doing it a new way. You are always alert and ready to "test and approve" your conviction and transformation to whatever is showing-up in your experience.

A while back, I remember hearing an old gospel song that was probably written before I was born but has been covered and redone by some remarkable gospel artists. It's a prayer really. The songwriter writes, "now Lord, don't move my mountain but give me the strength to climb. And Lord, don't take away my stumbling block but lead me all around." When the Hammond B-3 organ growls the melody and the instruments join in, feet start tapping, hands start clapping, and a good time is had by all. But in my transformed and renewed mind, this song makes no sense. As an avid fan of gospel music, specifically traditional gospel, my ears enjoy its distinguished and unique sound and beat, complimented by the skills of a trained soloist. But not even the best of soloists could help reconcile the lyrics of this song in my mind. Here is why.

In Matthew 21:22-25 New American Bible Revised Edition (NABRE), Jesus said, "Have faith in God. Truly I tell you, if anyone says to this mountain, be lifted up and thrown into the sea, and has no doubt in his heart, and believes that it will happen, it will be done for him. Whatever you ask in prayer, believe that you have received it, and it will be yours." We make a mistake of limiting God, therefore we have limitations and restrictions in our experience. When you tell God not to move your mountain, you are telling Him that you know He can but won't, which is a foolish and unnecessary thing to do. It's like saying, Lord, don't take away the condition, just help me endure the pain. Don't give me a job but just help me make it week by week without an income. It's like me saying to Dr. Michelle, don't cut and sew the problem away, just give me a higher strength pain medication as I pray against addiction. What if David had said to God, don't kill Goliath just help me endure the fight and battle? Sounds silly doesn't it? It's sad that this type of limited thinking occurs in the minds of believers and non-believers all day, every day, all around the world.

But I've got more good news. We, the transformed, the spiritually free, the truth-based believers continue to "test and approve" that God is good. And we know for sure that His will for us is good, pleasing and perfect.

To change the way you think and the way you've always thought about anything can be a struggle and can incite a battle in your mind and body between the old and new you. The scripture says, "test as well as approve." Testing comes through practice. When challenges show-up, you must boldly face them with this truth. Remember, once David came into truth, he ran <u>toward</u> the giant with boldness, fearlessness, and confidence. That's what you and I must do on this road to transformation.

To help us steady the course, I've culled out these <u>Nine Statements of Conviction.</u> These are examples of affirmations, introduced in the last chapter. These declarations are powerful tools to cement in our minds what it means to trust God the good in all situations. Read them aloud and commit to them. Make them personal, inserting your name. Strengthen and expand your conviction to this new way of thinking. And if they don't work for you (too long, too many etc.) create your own. Remember, this walk is personal. Make it your own.

Larry's Nine Statements of Conviction

I know for sure that:

1. **I am worthy of God's good** – I don't need to be a certain age, color, sexual orientation or member of a particular church to receive good from the Father. God is my Father and because He is my Father, I am heir to all the good that is pressed out of

Him. "The Lord is good to all; He has compassion on all He has made,"(Psalms 145:9 NIV).

2. **God is the source of all good** – There are many channels by which I receive my good (e.g., jobs, gifts, profits from a business, etc.). But these channels will come and go. God, however, is not a channel and as such, will never go away or close. He is the flowing spring of all good. "Every good and perfect gift is from above, coming down from the Father of the heavenly lights, who does not change like shifting shadows," (James 1:17 NIV).

3. **I am to have the best** – I live in a world of lavish abundance. Living an abundant life means that I don't have to settle for less than the very best the universe has available. I am drawn to the best of everything and it comes to me from the Father. "The thief cometh not but for to steal, and to kill, and to destroy - I am come that they might have life and that they might have it more abundantly," (John 10:10-King James Version KJV).

4. **I trust in and depend on God** – I know that in this human experience, I will encounter stressors, challenges and trouble. These conditions are temporary as they are contrary to what God wants for me. So, I depend on God to see me through every stressor, challenge and troubling situation. He will protect me. He will protect my soul. "The Lord is good and a stronghold in the day of trouble; and He knows those who trust Him," (Nahum 1:7 New King James Version-NKJV).

5. **It pleases God to bless me** – God is at the ready to unleash his good to me. He has designed the universe to create channels to receive. I thank God for what He has done, what He's doing, and His plans for my abundant future. "Fear not little flock, for your Father's good pleasure is to give you the kingdom," (Luke 12:32 KJV).

6. **He prospers not punishes** – I am God's perfect creation. When He made me, He appraised his work as good and very good; therefore, I reject any thoughts of being punished, hurt or harmed by God. My Father loves and cherishes me. "For I know the plans I have for you, declares the Lord; plans to prosper you and not

harm you, plans to give you hope and a future," (Jeremiah 29:11 NIV).

7. **God brings good to all situations** – When I make a mess of things, I count on God to help me clean it up. And when He appears, He not only cleans up my mess, He blesses me. "And we know that in all things, God works for the good of those who love Him, who have been called according to his purpose," (Romans 8:28 NIV).

8. **I give God the credit for all my good** – I know that God is good and all good is an output from God. When I receive, I do not attribute my good to the channel, rather, I give credit and thanks to God for keeping His promise. I recognize and thank Him for his favor. "Give thanks to the Lord for He is good; his love endures forever," (Psalms 107:1 NIV).

9. **Good is mine for the asking** – I know that anything to my highest good is mine if I ask God, believe in his favor, and do not doubt. "Therefore, I tell you, whatever you ask in prayer, believe that you have received it and it will be yours," (Mark11:24 NIV).

Think on These Things

1. What is your understanding of God's nature? Is it possible that He can be wrathful and good? Explain.

2. What do you think Paul meant when he wrote, "do not conform to the patterns of this world?"

3. What do you think it means to "test and approve" God's perfect will?

4. What makes us worthy of God's good?

5. Why is it important to "believe that you have received" in order for God to hear and attend to your prayer/request?

CHAPTER 3

I Am Masterfully Made

• • ● • •

"The Lord God formed man of the dust of the ground and breathed the breath of life into his nostrils and man became a living soul," (Genesis 2:7 NIV).

Have you ever stopped to think about yourself and how you are made? How the cells, tissue, and bones work in your body? How the engine of your body, the heart, pumps without a battery or power source other than God? Isn't it amazing that your body has an internal healing process to allow cuts, bruises, and abrasions to heal on their own? How is it that every nanosecond, your brain is sending messages to your body, enabling you to move your limbs to walk, stand, and sit? And how you automatically blink your eyes, lubricating your lenses and enhancing your ability to see clearly, near or far? Think about the construct of your body. Can you imagine your eyes, nose, or ears located anywhere else on your body? Every feature and placement of your organs was divinely and purposefully designed and planned. No other species or living thing is like us. Birds of the air, beasts of the ground, fish of the sea, though strong and mighty, do not compare to the perfection of man and how he was masterfully made. Because man was created by God and in the image and likeness of God, man, therefore, is perfect. We, therefore, are God's perfect creation.

In full disclosure, I have to admit that I struggled with thinking of myself as God's perfect anything. This comes from a constant comparison to images we see of beauty and perfection. A feeling of "less than" is resultant of this comparison. Women compare their curves and figures to those of superstars. Men compare their physique and fitness to those of muscular and viral athletes. It's natural to do so. We see those people as models and examples of perfection and that's what we want for ourselves. But as we learn about ourselves as students of truth, we learn that our perfection or image/likeness has less to do with what's on the outside than what is within.

In 2008, I joined a congregation of like-minded believers known as Christ Universal Temple (CUT). CUT was founded in 1956 by the late Reverend Dr. Johnnie Colemon as a church in the Unity network of churches and centers. After years as a Unity Church, Dr. Colemon established the Universal Foundation for Better Living (UFBL). CUT is a part of UFBL with the mission of teaching people how to live happy, prosperous, and healthy lives. Even after Dr. Colemon made her transition, CUT remains the flagship church of UFBL with thousands of members domestically and abroad. CUT has a strong teaching mission and ministry, offering a variety of courses through the Johnnie Colemon Institute (JCI). People from various churches and denominations attend classes at JCI because of its reputation of quality bible-based New Thought instruction.

I remember attending my first JCI course, Basic Truth Principles 1 with Dr. Emma Luster-Lassiter. I walked into the crowded classroom and nervously took a seat in the back row. Sure, I had attended spiritual development classes before, even taught a few, but something was telling me that this course was going to challenge me in ways that I've never been challenged before.

After introductions and prayer, Emma, short and petite in stature, turned to the chalk board and drew a large circle, requiring her to stand on her tip-toes to complete. She said, "in the beginning, God gathered radiant substance and formed it and breathed into it the breath of life, and man became a living soul." She went on to say that man was a three-fold being; Spirit, Mind and Body. The key to understanding God and your relationship with God was to also understand yourself. Over the next ten weeks, I was introduced to a body of spiritual knowledge that I had never heard before. I moved from the back row to the front. My hand was up regularly with questions and challenges to what I was learning.

How empowering to know that I am God's perfect creation not because of outward appearance but because of the qualities, nature, and attributes of my existence. When God breathed his breath into me, I became fully-equipped and able to handle all that I needed to handle in this life experience. I was loving this class. My mind was being renewed. I was glad to hear and accept the truth that I was made in His image and likeness and understood what that really meant. When old thinking and teachings that I once held as truths popped up, I rejected them. I was not a filthy rag to God; I was not a worm of the dust; I was not a poor pilgrim passing through a barren land. In reality, I was none of those things. I was built to be a conqueror, a master, a powerhouse. I am, we are three-fold masterfully made perfect creations of God.

Spirit

The very essence of our being is Spirit. The Spirit of God resides in each one of us. As children of God, that is something we all have in common. Spirit is not an outside force that moves inward, rather an inside state of pure being that expresses outward. I struggled with this new thought because my mind immediately focused on people who were dishonest, unethical, violent, and unscrupulous in their affairs and relationships. If they were true spiritual beings, how could they operate continually with intent to harm?

When my Basic Truth Principle classmates and I posed this question in class, Emma went to her bag. I thought to myself, what could she possibly have in that bag to answer this question. She pulled out a deflated balloon and said, "in the beginning, God gathered radiant substance, and formed it, and blew the breath of life into its nostrils and man became a living soul." She then filled the balloon with air and held it up before the class. "Without the breath of life," she said, "man would not exist. It wasn't until God breathed life into man that he had life. She then released the air from the balloon. She continued, "whether we like it or not, man cannot exist without the Spirit of God within." The balloon represented the gathering of radiant substance or as most of us have learned, dust. The air represented the decision and movement of God, pouring Himself into this formation of radiant substance. When the Spirit leaves the substance, the substance no longer exists. The message and lesson were clear. Every individual is walking, breathing, existing because of the Spirit of God within. What we as believers and followers of our Wayshower, Jesus the Christ must learn is how to leverage our "Spirit-self," in our pursuit of life and that more abundantly. Those who choose to be dishonest, unethical, violent, and unscrupulous simply have not come into the awareness of their spirit-self.

The God Spirit within expresses as we allow it to express. Some are ever expressing while others suppress expressing. Those who suppress or choose not to express (due to a lack of awareness or simply an unwillingness) choose, by default, to suffer or unnecessarily endure a life of sorrow, pain, and strife. This is not the will of God for his children and does not emulate his image nor his likeness.

In William Warch's book, *The New Thought Christian,* he explains it this way:

> Spirit is that God-like part of you which is the identical image and likeness of God. It is the invisible essence of you comprised of faith, strength, judgment, love, power, imagination, understanding, will order, zeal, renunciation, and life. This Spirit phase of you is God in you and commonly referred to as the Christ in you. Your Christ self is perfect and unchangeable. The New Thought Christian knows that the Christ resides within. They also know that the Christ is in everyone (Warch, 13).

I believe the key to cooperating and working with others is inner-nested in this awareness of the Christ in ourselves and in all.

Now I'm not delusional by any stretch of the imagination. I know it can be difficult at times to get along and cooperate with others for a myriad of reasons. Some people are not at the level of awareness to express or even understand the Christ within. Quite frankly, some people just don't like being around other people. They don't want to be bothered. With friends, family members, co-workers, old bosses and even fellow church folks, I've learned to "agree quickly with my adversaries" as scripture says for my own peace which is the most important. The key to a good relationship or interaction with these people is what I call the "Christ-to-Christ" approach. With this approach, we learn to look past appearances and what we are receiving through our senses to find and connect with the Christ Spirit in our brother or sister. There is an affirmation I was taught years ago when I was a member of the Spiritual church. It simply affirms that "the Christ in me beholds the Christ in you and the forgiving love of Jesus the Christ, fills my mind and heart, and I am at peace with God and man."

Mind

I liken the mind to the core processing unit (CPU) of a computer. Your mind, in essence, is the CPU of your being. Sometimes referred to as the soul or heart, the mind gathers, processes and stores information relative to everything you experience in your life.

There are three phases of mind: the Christ mind, the Conscious phase of mind, and the subconscious phase mind.

The Christ Mind in you is always connected to the Christ Spirit within, which is connected to Divine or Universal mind, which is God. We are masterfully designed to be led and guided by Divine mind, 24 hours a day, seven days a week, 365 days a year. When people say, "I have a hunch, or "something told me," or "I followed my first mind," what they are really saying is that they paid attention to the voice of the Christ within. Although I believe in prophets, seers, and those who have psychic ability, I firmly posit that prophets, seers, and psychics are not required or necessary to hear from God. You were masterfully made to hear and listen to the Christ in you for warnings, instructions, and information directly from Divine Mind.

In May 1990, I accepted a human resources position in Madison, Wisconsin for a major insurance company. I was to train and live in Madison for one year and then relocate to the Chicagoland area to work in the Schaumburg, Illinois office. Ramona and I planned on getting married after my stent in Madison, but the separation was harder than either of us imagined, so in August 1990, we married, and she joined me in Madison. The following March, I was officially informed that I would begin working in Schaumburg on June 1. This meant that we had about three months to find a place to live. This was a major challenge for us as our credit was abysmal and our savings, well we didn't have any. We were extremely concerned, particularly being a one-income household as Ramona only worked part-time retail in Madison and had not secured a job in Chicago. I knew inside my mind that things were going to work out. How they were going to work out was, however, the concern. In my mind, I envisioned us in a beautiful two-story town home in the suburbs, blocks from my soon-to-be new office. My finances had a different vision – more like a one-bedroom apartment in the inner-city in a not-so-safe neighborhood, miles and miles away from Schaumburg. But faith without works is dead, so we ventured full speed ahead.

On Saturdays after payday when we could afford it, we'd travel from Madison to the Schaumburg area in search of an apartment. I can still remember the anxiety and the thump in my stomach when we'd exit the highway to the bottom of the ramp and then make that right turn toward apartment complexes in Schaumburg and Arlington Heights. We toured some beautiful properties, but with one guaranteed income and less than stellar credit, no one would rent to us.

On one house hunting trip, we were in our usual position, at the light at the bottom of the ramp, full of nervousness and anxiety, ready to make that right-hand turn. But something happened. Ramona said, "turn left. We always turn right, but let's go left this time and see what's down there." I agreed and we turned left. The very first complex we saw was Williamsburg Town Homes and Apartments. We looked at each other with cautious excitement. Driving onto the property, we saw rows and rows of two-story town homes for rent, with a few apartments in the middle of the complex. We immediately dismissed the town homes as an option, assuming that we couldn't afford them.

We walked into the rental office and asked for a tour of the apartment model. A bright and vivacious woman named Pam greeted us and shook our hands. She then said, "wouldn't you prefer a town home? We are upgrading all our town homes with new appliances and carpeting and if you sign a lease before May 1st, you'll be eligible for a $1,500 rebate after three months." I shook my head indicating no, but Ramona said, "yes." I was annoyed because I didn't want to see them, fall in love with them, and then get denied, but I went along with the program. Again faith without works is dead. Pam put us on a golf cart and took us to the town home model. It was perfect for us, complete with a large master bedroom and a small fenced-in patio and backyard. My entire disposition changed. I had to come to myself. God was in the process of giving me what I had envisioned. I stopped thinking impossible and started seeing the possibilities.

We went back to the office and completed the application. I informed Pam of our current financial situation. I also offered to waive the $1,500 rebate in exchange for an approved application. She said, "that's just silly. We look at more than credit when evaluating an application. There are some people with perfect credit who we would never rent to and people with terrible credit who we'd rent to in a heartbeat. I can tell just by working with you two that you would be great renters. Let's not worry about the application. Let's just make sure you like the place." We laughed and played it off but after we left Pam, that's exactly what we did – until we let it go. We knew there was no more for us to do but depend on God. Pam said we'd have a decision in a week. We spent three days suppressing our worry and anxiety, leaving it up to God and that's when something strange happened. On that Tuesday as I prayed, I heard God say, "approved." From that point on, I focused on that word in everything I did. It seemed to jump out of the sentence in every newspaper, magazine or document I picked-up that day. Even television commercials flashed "approved" when under normal circumstances, I probably wouldn't have paid attention. My anxiety turned to excitement as I continued imagining myself in that town home.

On Wednesday morning, Pam called me at work with the good news. We were approved; however because of our credit, we had to pay a double-deposit and first month's rent, which equated to about $2,400. I thanked her. She cautioned me to hurry because the units were moving fast. We needed to come in as soon as possible and put down the deposit to hold the unit we wanted. I informed Ramona who was excited and relieved to hear the good news. I asked her where in the "heck" are we gonna come up with that money by the weekend? She told me that it would all work out and not to worry. We hadn't come this far to lose out now.

Later that afternoon, my boss asked me if we had found a place and I told him yes, but they need a security deposit right away, like this weekend. He told me that the company would pay for the moving of our household items and give me a relocation allowance equal to six weeks of pay after the move was completed. This was great news. I called Pam back to see what we could work out. She said to bring a letter from my employer guaranteeing the relocation allowance and amount, give her a predated check, and $100 in cash. This would hold the apartment for us. On June 1st, we were in our new upgraded town home and because of a clerical error, we were given the larger town home at the smaller townhome rent. We used our returned security deposit from our apartment in Madison (which I'd forgotten about) to buy a few pieces of furniture and our $1,500 rebate to pay some bills. And for an added blessing, Ramona started her new job in her chosen field just a few days after we moved. All this fortune and favor came by listening to the Christ Mind within. What I really wanted but dismissed as impossible was possible and already done. I know for sure that He will give you the desires of your heart. I know for sure that God has designed the universe to bring forth everything I desire that is to my highest good. I know worry and anxiety were not things He breathed into me when I was created and therefore don't resemble Him in any way. Facts may speak or suggest one thing, but nothing and no one can stop God the good from being God the good. This is just one of so many examples where He has spoken instructions, directions, and answers to my heart. And I am careful to attribute my blessings to Him with praise and thanksgiving.

The Conscious Mind is where we process and evaluate all the information we receive primarily from our senses: what we hear, see, touch, taste and smell. It's in the conscious mind that thinking (movement of ideas in the mind) occurs. Here we apply intelligence and logic to our thoughts to reason and make decisions. Facts, details and proof are very important to our conscious phase of mind as they help us make simple to complicated decisions.

Unfortunately it is due in part to the conscious phase that we make our biggest mistakes. When thoughts and ideas come to us from the Christ Mind, we often ignore them. In Emile Cady's book, *"Lessons in Truth,"* she introduces the term mortal mind.

> Mortal mind, the term so much used and so distracting to many, is the error consciousness, which gathers its information from the outside world through the five senses. It is what Paul calls the mind of the flesh in contradiction to spiritual mind; and he flatly says: The mind of the flesh [believing what the carnal mind says] is death [sorrow, trouble, sickness]; but the mind of the Spirit [ability to still the carnal mind and let the Spirit speak within us] is life and peace (Cady, 22).

This mortal mind is comfortable with lack and limitation and makes us feel comfortable in thinking ourselves out and away from what we glean from the Christ Mind. It is critical to your understanding and transformation that you eliminate this dynamic from your experience. If we accept the idea of God as the essence and source of all good, we must accept that information from the Christ Mind has been vetted and deemed brilliant and perfect and does not require us to question.

I love it when I hear people say and take credit for "the best idea they ever had." The reality is you have never had an original idea (to your highest good) before in your life. All great ideas from the invention of the telephone to the internet and those great ideas to come are from God the good omnipotent. God is done creating. He does not need to create another thing. God, through the Christ Mind, will give us, warnings, instructions and million-dollar ideas that if pursued, will lead to abundant living, peace of mind, and perfect health. As truth-based believers, we must learn how to discern his voice and move as He guides and directs us. We must come into the awareness to know that when we follow the leading of the Christ, we cannot make a mistake, nor can we fail because we have unshakable faith and trust in the Christ within. It is critical to your spiritual freedom that you are able to use your conscious phase of mind to accept and follow the leading of the Lord and not ignore them or push them away.

The Subconscious Mind is where every thought, feeling, and experience you have ever had is stored. Some characterize the subconscious (or below conscious) as a tape recorder that captures all experiences and plays them back during thinking whether we want it to or not. I think of the subconscious as a filing cabinet with folders that store all the good, bad, and "lack-luster" thoughts and experiences of our lives. And at the precise time I'm thinking or deliberating a decision, the file is pulled up and all the details flow to my conscious phase of mind, often in contradiction to my Christ mind. I believe this is what the Apostle Paul meant when he said, "For we wrestle not against flesh and blood but against principalities, against powers, against rulers of the darkness of the world, against spiritual wickedness in high places," (Ephesians 6:12 KJV). The principalities are all the facts and details and opinions you have stored in your subconscious phase of mind. And these facts, details, and opinions wrestle with the perfect good news messages of your Christ mind. In the conscious phase, the struggle occurs between God-given ideas and thoughts and the application of the facts from past information or experiences filed in our subconscious.

Earlier in our marriage, we were blessed to get Ramona the car of her dreams: The Ford Expedition Eddie Bauer Edition. She was so excited at the dealership to the point that she couldn't drive it home. Back then, I drove a much smaller car (compared to hers) which was old and wrought with all kinds of mechanical problems, but it started and got me from point A to point B safely. I convinced myself to be satisfied, knowing that

I would get my dream car in the future when I had convinced myself that it was affordable.

As the weeks passed, the thought of a new car kept showing-up in my mind. God was giving me a divine idea. I had dreams where I was signing papers and being handed keys from the salesperson at the dealership. But whenever I'd think about a new car, the files in my subconscious would pill up thoughts that kept me from pursing this idea that I discovered was from God. Thoughts of:

- Fear - remembering how embarrassed I was when I applied for a car loan and wasn't approved;
- Doubt – I just bought a new car for Ramona. There is no way Ford will approve another loan;
- Envy –Maybe I'm just jealous because Ramona has a new car and I don't;
- Limitation – I cannot afford another car note right now; and
- Mortal – face the facts, I have no money for another car.

So I did what I normally did and what some of you normally do; I let that idea go away, so I thought.

One evening, I took my daughters out for some daddy-daughter time. They were toddlers then and full of energy. We went to Old Country Buffet, got our food and sat in a booth by the window. As we were eating, the car idea resurfaced. I heard "go to the dealership, I'll watch the girls." I looked at my watch and it was after 7:00 p.m. I then looked across the table at my girls and thought, there is no way. I then heard, "when you hear my voice, don't harden your heart." I paid a bit more attention, but it was God through Jesseca that got me to move. Looking out of the window she said, "Daddy, look. It's mommy's car. It's the same color and everything. You need a new car like mommy's." I told them to hurry and finish. We were going to the look at cars. They were more excited than I was – that's for certain.

Now when I think about the look on the salesman's face when we walked in, I can laugh about it. He came quickly towards me with a look of grave concern. "Mr. Robertson," he said, "is something wrong with your Expedition?" I replied no and told him I had this crazy idea of buying a Ford Explorer for myself. I didn't want a used one. I wanted a new one, complete with that new car smell. I told him that I was just looking because I had the kids with me. By this time, the ice cream and Old Country Buffet desserts started kicking in. The girls were chasing each other in a circle with me in the middle. My salesman said, "my daughter will watch your kids. I hired her to provide childcare for parents while going through the process. There are three other kids with her now, playing and watching a movie."

That evening, right before the dealership closed, I drove my new fire-engine red Ford Explorer (aka Cora) off the lot. I drove up to the house and called Ramona. She came out with her mouth agape in pure disbelief. We went for a quick drive and returned home. She just shook her head and laughed. We prayed and thanked God for speaking and making a way out of what appeared to be no way.

I learned through this experience that nothing, not even my below-conscious thinking, could stop God from working in my life. Dr. Colemon used to say that "it works if you work it." I'm a witness that it works even if you don't work it. But what if we were able to work it? What if we were able to control this "wrestling" in our soul to hear God and only God? What if we were able to rid our "high place" of all the experiences, examples, thoughts, feelings, fears, envy, lack, and limitation? What if we moved in consciousness from a fact-based existence to a truth-based life?

I have learned and am still learning through practice to control my thinking and all the information that enters into my mind. I gravitate to positive energy. I surround myself with people who are positive and "up focused" rather than "down focused." I trust God to give me guidance, direction, signs, and wonders toward my highest good. I'm in tune and obedient to his voice and his voice only. I know for sure that "greater is He (invisible intelligent energy) that is within me than he that is in the world," (1 John 4:4 KJV).

Body

Your body can be described as the clothing or covering of your spirit and soul. In 1st Corinthians 6:19 NIV, Paul said in his letter to the people at Corinth, "Do you not know that your bodies are temples of the Holy Spirit, who is in you, whom you have received from God? You are not your own." Our bodies are masterfully made to express and demonstrate the nature, qualities, and characteristics of God. Your body is a giant television screen, expressing your beliefs, thoughts, feelings and level of consciousness development. That's why Christians with a cultivated relationship with God can quickly and accurately discern the consciousness of others just by observing and listening. It's greater and more profound than a "first impression," because first impressions rely solely on appearances. The Spiritual discernment I'm describing is only relative to an understanding of how the Christ is being expressed outwards. When you come into contact or conversation with another person and you hear the still small voice say, "something is not quite right," that is spiritual discernment.

Our bodies complete the trinity of our being: spirit, mind and body, therefore it is incumbent upon us to take care of our body temples. Our spirit and soul will only occupy our bodies to the extent that it can. Observing a healthy lifestyle that includes a healthy diet, exercise, exceptional hygiene, skin care and moderation in everything we do, improves the body's ability to serve as a temple for our spirit and soul. We know at some point in our time, our bodies will not be able to hold our spirit, thus we will need to give-up our bodies and transition back to pure being. That does not mean death because the real us cannot die – it's Spirit.

One of the milestones of my spiritual journey was the day I understood and accepted that I was masterfully created in the image and likeness of God. It was a truth that required some heavy mental lifting because the concept was foreign to me and flew in the face of the fundamental doctrines I was taught. As an expression of God or as a child of God, there are some things about me that are similar to my Father. In this experience, some tell me I look like my mother. Others say I favor my father. It isn't a surprise because I was created through them. It shouldn't be surprising to you to resemble God, your Father and creator.

When God breathed the breath of life into man, and man became a living soul, man inherited the powers he needed to survive spiritually and physically. These powers resemble the attributes, qualities, and nature of God, and have been expressed through man from Abraham to Jesus. I learned them as the *Twelve Powers of Man*.

In his classic book, *The Twelve Powers of Man*, Unity Church co-founder, Charles Fillmore, describes the innate powers we all have that when called upon or expressed, can lead us to better living and an abundant life. The primary scriptural reference for this work is found in Matthew 19:28; "verily I say unto you that ye who have followed me, in the regeneration when the Son of man shall set on the throne of his glory, ye also shall sit upon twelve thrones, judging the twelve tribes of Israel. And everyone that hath left houses, or brethren, or sisters, or fathers, or mothers, or children, or lands for my name's sake, shall receive a hundredfold, and shall inherit eternal life." Fillmore aligns these twelve powers with the twelve disciples Jesus calls unto Him. As we are developing spiritually, we train and awaken deeper and larger powers, sending our thoughts down and through our whole selves for action. Fillmore says,

> "When Jesus Christ had attained a certain soul development, He called His twelve disciples to Him. This means that when man is developing out of mere personal consciousness into spiritual consciousness, he begins to train deeper and larger powers; he sends his thoughts down into the inner centers of his organism, and through his word, quickens them to life. Where before his powers have worked in the personal, now they begin to expand and work in the universal. This is the first and the second coming of Christ, spoken of in the scriptures. The first coming is the receiving of Truth into the conscious mind, and the second coming is the awakening and

the regeneration of the subconscious mind through the
Christ mind (Fillmore, 15).

The powers are presented in our bodies and are expressed by us in a
number of ways. These powers are not foreign to even the casual believer.
Their worth and potency comes from how they are used and expressed
in our existence and experience. *The Twelve Powers*, name of the disciples
that align with each and the location in our body is outlined in the chart
below:

Power	Disciple Alignment	Location in the Body
Faith	Peter	Center of the brain
Strength	Andrew	Loins
Judgement	James	Stomach
Love	John	Back of the Heart
Power	Phillip	Root of the Tongue
Imagination	Bartholomew	Between the Eyes
Understanding	Thomas	Front Brain
Will	Matthew	Center front Brain
Order	James	Navel
Zeal	Simon	Back of the Head
Elimination	Thaddeus	Abdominal Region
Life	Judas	Generative Function

The journey in developing expertise and understanding of this
teaching is personal. It requires a gleaning that you can only get through
reading, studying, and practicing. I know for sure that this truth, though
different and somewhat esoteric, is transformational, enlightening, and
potent to the goal of your existence to express God and live a truth-based
abundant life.

As masterfully made creations, it pleases God when we see, believe,
and present ourselves as He sees us. There is a beautiful worship song
written by Reuben Morgan entitled *Give Thanks* that affirms, "let the
weak say I am strong, let the poor say I am rich, let the blind say I can
see, it's what the Lord has done in me." True deliverance is moving from

how we see ourselves to how God sees us: His perfect masterfully-made creation.

Think on These Things

1. If God is not a man but everywhere present Spirit intelligence, how are we created in His image and likeness?
2. What are the three phases of mind? Which phase is likened to a tape recorder or file cabinet?
3. Complete this statement: Man became a living soul after _____.
4. Why is spiritual discernment more profound than a "first impression?"
5. You have never had a great idea in your life. Explain why/how this statement is true.

CHAPTER 4

His Yoke Is Easy

• ● ● ● •

> *"Come to me, all you who are weary and burdened, and I
> will give you rest. Take my yoke upon you and learn from me,
> for I am gentle and humble in heart, and you will find rest
> for your souls. For my yoke is easy and my burden is light,"*
> *(Matthew 11: 28-30 NIV).*

I want to start this fourth chapter talking about a friend of mine we'll
call Oscar. Oscar is a young man I met on a train ride from DC to New
York last Spring. We were in business class and had the fortune of having
just about the first section of the car to ourselves. From across the aisle,
we struck-up a conversation and casually discussed everything from the
antics of our current president to our respective shoe collections and
how difficult it could be finding our shared size 13. I could tell from his
overall disposition and vocabulary that Oscar was an intelligent and
accomplished professional. He was a marketing manager for a medical
device company in New York but lived in D.C. We had a great time until
we broached the subject of religion. They say you should never discuss
religion and politics but since we had talked about everything else,
religion was a logical next discussion topic. The conversation turned
very serious and somber.

I told him where I attended church. He smiled and affirmed that he
knew my church and pastor and was very complimentary, referring to my

minister as his internet pastor. When I asked him where he worshiped, his response was interesting and the reason why this chapter is in the book.

Oscar told me about his disdain for church in great detail. He was raised Catholic and attended, like me, Catholic school through the 12th grade. He said, he really didn't think too much about his spiritual life while he was young. He did what he thought he was supposed to do which was go to mass on Sundays, sell raffle tickets, help out with Bingo on Saturday nights, and pretty much do whatever else the priests and nuns told him to do.

While in college, he visited a Pentecostal church with his then girlfriend. He remembered vividly being confused as to why she was taking her bible to church. He joked, saying that it was a waste of time because the minister or priest would read the scriptures aloud anyway. She informed him that the Pentecostal church did not have priests. Afterwards, not only did she take her bible, she found another one and gave it to him, so he would be prepared for church. He loved the music and the charismatic vibe. He continued going and a few months later, he joined. His girlfriend was very excited. She shouted and spoke in tongues, which was still strange to him. But it was not an issue for him. He said somewhere between the cold and stoic Catholic mass and the shake, rattle and roll of the Pentecostals, there was room for him.

By the time he graduated from college, he was an active member and lead singer in the choir. He had become accustomed to all the activities and rituals and participated accordingly. He wore white on first Sundays, was always dressed conservatively, never entering the sanctuary, even for choir rehearsal without either a jacket or tie, sometimes both. He fell in love with his church. The people were generally friendly and authentic and somewhat judgmental but, in his mind, all church folks were judgmental.

One Sunday after service, one of the elders pulled him to the side for a chat. The elder said that he was concerned because in all the years he'd been attending, he never saw Oscar encounter the Holy Ghost. He questioned Oscar's salvation, which in turn made Oscar begin to question his salvation himself. He explained to the elder that he felt God in a quiet and personal way and that shouting and speaking in tongues was not his thing. He told his wife about his conversation, knowing that she would be outraged at the nerve of the elder. Surprisingly, his wife agreed with the elder and said others had discussed the same concern. Oscar said he prayed, read his bible and knew how to worship and felt good about his spiritual life. He had come a long way since the Roman Catholic experience and was content in his current conviction, but obviously, that was not good enough for everyone else.

A few Sundays later, the elder pulled him aside again to check on him. Oscar shared that his wife and a few other folks in the church had the same concern. The elder then suggested that he learn how to do the "holy dance" and speak in tongues saying that eventually the Spirit would "jump on him" and he'd be truly saved. So Oscar practiced dancing, and he listened to others speak in tongues. One Sunday, he tried it and it just felt fake and phony and for good reason – it was. He got great reactions from folks in the choir and congregation including his wife and the elder, but he knew it wasn't real. People even remarked to him that they were glad that his salvation had finally come. His wife was ecstatic. He joked that it wasn't coincidental that soon thereafter she was pregnant with their first child. We shared a big laugh about his inuendo-weighted comment.

A year or so later, while he was pretending to dance, he had an epiphany. How could God be pleased with him and how could He be pleased with some other people (no doubt) doing the same thing? If he was pretending, how many others were pretending? He started questioning the customs and the rituals and scanning his bible for proof that all the outer pageantry was even necessary. The uniform and the dress code, and you can't do this, and you can't do that, and the fake dancing and tongue speaking was just habit and routine. Something was wrong.

He became so conflicted that he sought out his pastor for counsel and that's when it happened. When Oscar told his pastor that he felt phony and conflicted, his pastor in turn told him that he had been tricked by the devil who was trying to take him off the straight and narrow. He explained that the elder and his wife were trying to help and lead him to Christ, but his resistance was a sign that his mind and spirit had been compromised by the devil. The next Sunday, his pastor pulled him out of the choir, placed him in the middle of a circle of ministers and elders and performed what he called an exorcism of sorts. He was so embarrassed and humiliated, things you shouldn't feel in church. He said he just stood there in the circle, angry and ashamed. "The tears that were rolling down my face were not tears of joy." Afterwards the pastor told him that he couldn't sing in the choir again until he got himself right with God. His wife didn't support him. She was embarrassed that she was married to a man who had been compromised by the devil. Oscar left that Sunday and never went back. He found a Catholic church and started attending regularly but his spirit remained unsettled. He ended-up watching church on television on Sundays. He said that was the safest way to worship – above reproach, criticism and embarrassment, and in the privacy of his own home, wearing whatever he wanted to wear and not being forced into antics that were disingenuous. He joked, saying, "a half-hour with Joel [Osteen] was all I needed."

His marriage didn't last for a myriad of reasons, the aforementioned being only one. He has two children now, one attended church with the mother and the other in front of the television with him. I, of course, invited him to my church, but he refused. He said the Baptist are wrong because they believe this, and the Methodist are wrong because they believe that. He went down a list of denominations and articulated his issues with each one. He says he meditates, prays, treats people right, sends his offerings electronically and stays home on Sundays. He said, "I know you probably think it is an excuse, but the church has put a bad taste in my mouth, not about God but about organized religion. I don't need a go between. I can talk to and worship God in the comfort of my own home with Joel and Victoria [Osteen]." I tried my best to minister to him, but his experience would not let him receive anything I had to say. He said that he didn't understand why church folks had to make God so complicated and complicated to the point of apathy. He said, "God is easy, it's church and church folks that's hard."

I began to think: how many Oscars are out in the world, wandering from doctrine to doctrine, church to church, telecast to telecast, unsure about their spiritual well-being? How many people are like Oscar, refusing to go to church in fear of ridicule, shaming, banishment or getting it wrong? How many people see salvation and freedom as confusing, arduous, and frightening? There is work to be done here. We, those with a relationship with God, must change this dynamic, which prevents people from worshiping in the beauty of assembly and collective consciousness. I think we have to start by changing our language, approach and demonstrations from arduous and long-suffering to graciousness and joy. From a God that is far-away and distant and hard to reach, to a God that is within us, closer than the fibers of our being. We've got to show ourselves and the Oscars of the world that church may be hard, but God is easy.

I, like many who will read this book, was raised to believe, fear, and obey God and his word. I learned that yes, there were some people who had not accepted God, didn't believe in God and wanted nothing to do with the belief of a "supreme being" or all the "God-stuff" that went along with it. I was taught to pray for these people because no matter how good their life was, it could be so much better with God. Some come to God through a calling from within to repent and walk a narrow way. Some come out of fear. After a life-threatening experience there are those who believe that God allowed them to go through and survive a horrific ordeal to get their attention. Some of our elders can tell us stories about a tarrying for God or spending days, weeks, months on the mourner's bench waiting for that stirring and awakening. No matter the motivation, orientation, or calling, it created a "born again experience," that changed our lives. But what about the non-believer? What about those who were not raised in a God-centered environment, or were not able to hear the calling from within? How do we bring these folks to their "born again experience?" Or for those who have strayed away or need to be renewed for whatever reason; how do we reach them? The older generation referred to these people as backsliders, intimating that they have "slid back" into their old "pre-saved" state. How do we compel them or facilitate the born-again experience?

In Matthew 11, Jesus makes it clear that the way to Him is easy and not complicated. Simply come unto me, He says, just as you are, right where you are (especially those who are burdened and tired) and "I will give you rest." I believe He's saying, you've tried so many ways to achieve the status of affluence, confidence, and peace and none of those ways worked. In fact, acting out this error-state of being has made you tired and has added to your burdens and weariness. Your futile attempts to attain a true peaceful mind fail over and over again. Imitating what you see as "the right way" has made you, like Oscar, tired and weary. Jesus is saying, because my Father and I are one, I have the agency and capacity to give you rest, the likes of which you have not seen. And don't worry about my load. My yoke (i.e., ability to walk with you and take in your stuff) is easy because I AM GOD, and no matter how much you give me as a burden (your stuff), my burdens are light. Learn of me and my ways and you can be free and free indeed. Simply, come unto me.

Coming unto God begins with a decision. In *Lessons in Truth,* Emily Cady begins her masterpiece with a very powerful assertion strategically positioned in the chapter title: "Bondage or Liberty, which?" At some point in this human experience, we have to choose between ourselves, dismissive of the Christ within (bondage) or expressing and demonstrating the Christ (liberty and freedom). We choose to suffer or embrace bondage when we forget how we've been masterfully made, as spiritual beings always connected to God. Dr. Cady writes,

> Man, who is at first, living in the selfish animal part of himself, will grow up through various stages and by various processes to the divine or spiritual understanding wherein he knows that he is one with the Father, and wherein he is free from all suffering because he has conscious dominion over all things. Somewhere on this journey, the human consciousness or intellect comes to a place where it gladly bows to its spiritual self and confesses that its spiritual self, its Christ, is highest and is Lord (Cady, 4).

In reality, I posit, you cannot have it wrong. How you embrace God and express Him in your way is a personal decision and covenant between you and God. I cannot believe nor do I accept that everyone has it wrong. According to my research, there are over 300 religions and denomination in the United States. How can some (entrenched in their denomination) wag the finger at the other 299 claiming to be right and others wrong? It's this stance and approach that makes God and salvation appear so complicated. You have some people who go to church on Saturdays. There are some who don't believe in musical instruments in the church. You have some who don't believe in water baptism or communion services. In some houses of worship, the women sit on one side and the men sit on the other. I heard a minister on television say, you cannot take communion in this church if you burn candles and incense. I said out loud to the television, who cares? As long as they are not worshiping candles and incense, what is it to thee? We've got to get God for ourselves. Paul declared, "that if you confess with your mouth the Lord Jesus and believe in your heart that God has raised Him from the dead, you will be saved," (Roman 10:9 NKJV). It's just that simple!

The decision is not a choice between heaven and hell (as places) or God and the devil (as powers in a constant fight for your soul). It's a choice to accept God and all that He is, working and expressing through you, his supreme creation or not. We make understanding God, salvation, and spiritual living so hard with our rituals, customs and traditions to the point God, salvation and spiritual living appear magical, mysterious and mystical. In our churches and assemblies and centers, we are so focused on what to wear, what not to wear, which isle to walk down, where to sit, etc. that we lose site of the purpose of church – GOD.

Secondly, coming unto God requires action. James wrote, "For as the body without the spirit is dead, so faith without works is dead also" (James 2:26 NKJV). Faith without works (action) means no change – nothing is new. Action is required to live in liberty and walk in this new consciousness and awareness. James isn't necessarily speaking of physical labor here. The works he speaks of are not a reference to joining church. We know that everything begins with consciousness (in the mind) so must these works begin. In order for salvation, transformation, and freedom to be expressed and demonstrated outwards, salvation, transformation and freedom have to be developed within.

One of the greatest lessons that illustrates this point is the Moses story. After Moses made the decision to come to the mountain to commune with God (the God Spirit within) and before he went to Pharaoh to demand freedom (dealt with files of his subconscious phase of mind) there were some actions he had to take to carve out even the possibility of freedom. Metaphysically, the actions of Moses illustrate the steps he had to take, and we have to take for deliverance and freedom. Let's examine these steps:

Come to God

> *"Now Moses was tending the flock of Jethro, his father-in-law, the priest of Medinan. And he led his flock to the back of the desert and came to Horeb, the mountain of God," (Exodus 3:1 NKJV).*

In the last chapter, I introduced the idea of the Christ mind within each one of us. Being led by the Christ within brings a spiritual guarantee of success as the voice of God will never harm nor lead us to harm. Moses coming to the mountain of God represents the attuning to the voice of the Christ Spirit within. Mountains, strong and high structures, can represent unmovable barriers, but here, they represent a high place in consciousness. Your Christ mind in sync with the Spirit part of your being is the highest state of being you can experience. It is in this state that assignments are given, questions are answered, and new masterful ideas are revealed. Moses' actions of coming to the high place illustrates this supreme level of awareness where there is happiness, health, and abundant living. And because this Spirit of God resides within, it's important to note that Moses didn't <u>go</u> to God, he <u>came</u> to God, which represents a turning and tuning within.

Trust God

> *"And the angel of the Lord appeared to him in the flame of fire out of the midst of a bush. So he looked and behold, the bush was burning with fire, but the bush was not consumed. Then Moses said, I will now turn aside to see this great sight, why the bush does not burn. When the Lord saw that he turned aside to look, God called to him from the midst of*

the bush, Moses, Moses, and he said, here I am," (Exodus
3:2-4 NKJV).

What Moses saw was unbelievable. Only God could set fire to a bush
and not allow it to burn. This was God's way of assuring Moses that his
efforts would be supported, co-signed, and underwritten by the full agency
and greatness of God. God wanted Moses, through this demonstration,
to know that He (God) had the power and ability to illuminate within
Moses the ideas and qualities of God. God demonstrates that He was
trustworthy because He had the power to do any and everything Moses
needed to be done in carrying out his assignment. This God that Moses
thought he knew was proving Himself to Moses all over again. From this
encounter, Moses would never be the same. In the days to come, when
Moses would get tired of going to Pharaoh time after time, he would recall
his burning bush experience and move boldly forward. He would reflect
on this experience as a reminder of the power he had to do anything
through and with God. Moses' response of "here I am" demonstrates his
readiness and acceptance of all that God is.

Separate Yourself

> *"Then He said, do not draw near this place. Take your*
> *sandals off your feet, for the place where you stand is holy*
> *ground," (Exodus 3:5 NKJV).*

In conducting research for this part of the book, I was overwhelmed
with the volumes of opinion and commentary about this scripture. The
opinions ranged from questionable to profound. What God gave me in
interpreting this scripture was simple. God needed Moses to understand
that in order to be successful in carrying out his assignment, he had to
transition from relying on what was familiar and ordinary (intellectual)
to things that were unfamiliar and challenging but possible with God
(spiritual). I posit that God needed him to understand that He was real,
holy, and sovereign and no-thing would be impossible through His
omniscience, omnipotence, and omnipresence. Moses would not be

successful relying on the facts understood through human consciousness. In order to be successful, he would have to rely on the truth that all things are possible with and through God. Moses had to separate himself from the old thoughts, beliefs, and assumptions and embrace the new. The ground (or his full awareness) was now holy.

Be Bold

> *"Come now, therefore and I will send you to Pharaoh that you may bring my people, the children of Israel out of Egypt. But Moses said to God, who am I that I should go to Pharaoh and that I should bring the children of Israel out of Egypt? So He said, I will certainly be with you. And this shall be a sign to you that I have sent you. When you have brought the people out of Egypt, you shall serve God on this mountain. Then Moses said to God, indeed, when I come to the children of Israel and say to them, the God of your father has sent me to you, and they say to me, what is His name, what shall I say to them? And God said to Moses, I Am who I Am, thus you shall say to the children of Israel, I Am has sent you," (Exodus 3:10-14 NKJV).*

Can you imagine yourself as Moses in this scenario? No, I'm not speaking of his inhibitions or his trepidation in confronting Pharaoh or in the mind-blowing challenge of convincing the ruler and grand slave master to give his tormented workforce freedom. I'm speaking of the confidence and boldness he must have had. Think about it: God Himself told him to go and He would be with him. This was the promise: whatever you endure, there is really no need to worry because God, the I Am is with you. Moses found confidence and assurance in this promise. It was through this confidence and assurance that He was able to confront Pharaoh over and over again, boldly demanding that the children of Israel be set free.

Moses' communion with God at Hobner represents the relationship and the interaction between the Spirit part of our being and our Christ mind. The interaction between Moses and Pharaoh represents the challenge of not allowing intellect and all the thoughts, feelings and experiences filed away in our subconscious phase of mind (our lower selves) to distract us, frighten us, or dissuade us from following the leadings of God. To have a happy, free, healthy and abundant life as children of God, we must be bold in our endeavors, knowing and trusting that the I Am is always with us to the manifestation of our success. If we could only develop the consciousness and awareness of our power and the power of the Spirit of God within, what challenge, what situation, what Goliath, what Pharaoh could ever defeat us?

We suffer because we choose to suffer. We suffer because we forget our divinity. We forget who we are, whose we are and how we were made. We forget our spiritual lineage. People who suffer cannot be bold. Suffering is evidence of error-thinking. It is the output of thoughts of lack, inferiority, and unworthiness. These thoughts did not manifest in our Christ mind, but from the lower caverns of ourselves. I'm sure Moses doubted himself, but he kept working on his assignment with the inner confidence in the one who sent him, the I Am God. I hear people say, "I'm living my best life" or "I am moving to the next level," and I'm intrigued. How are you going to do that? I see no evidence of effort, confidence, or boldness. What good is it to have God's promise and not stand on it? What is demonstrated is theatrical. What's heard is "sounding brass or tinkling cymbal," (1 Corinthians 13:1 KJV). Once you understand what you are and what you have the power to do, you have come to God and you are living to His glory. It may not always be easy, in fact it won't. It takes practice, but practicing what you know makes you a confident, bold, powerhouse child of God.

Linda Martella-Whitsitt describes this boldness as Divine Audacity. In her book of the same name, she explains that

> Divine Audacity is bold spiritual living, living under the radical premise that I Am divine. My nature is one with divine nature or God. I am able to boldly express the highest spiritual principles in the middle of everyday situations. I am courageously responsive. I am fearlessly

self-reflective and self-corrective. I am intentional in
large and small aims. I valiantly champion the goodness
within myself and within each person I encounter,
(Martell-Whitsett, 3).

I've learned to walk boldly without fear or hesitation. When I receive
a divine idea, I press on, I don't take no for an answer, I hold on to the
manifestation in my consciousness. Paul refers to this visioning faith as
the ability to "…calleth those things which be not as though they were,"
(Romans 4:17 KJV). Some may accuse me of being arrogant or working
with an ego that's out of control. Boldness in God is not ego. Boldness is
assurance, blessed assurance, and confidence in God. Ego is assurance
and confidence in self. Let's be clear – self-confidence and self-esteem are
important but not to the point where you subtract God from the equation.

Let me tell you about a young man who was an employee at one of
the organizations I worked. We'll call him Marcus. One morning, Marcus
came into my office with a manila file folder in his hand. We sat at my
conference table and removed all the documents from his folder. He said,
"Mr. Larry, I'm about to tell you a story." He began to go through each
document, illustrating his accomplishments and performance since he
began his career with the organization. At the conclusion of his story, he
informed me that because he had performed well above expectations,
it was time for him to be promoted. I explained to him that promotions
are not considered from employees directly, but from the employee's
manager. I explained that as his human resources director, I appreciated
the story and his hard work, but it was his manager that he needed to
persuade first. He said that he shared his story with his manager months
ago and nothing has happened. He was coming to me for my help. I was
unable to help him. I couldn't circumvent his manager nor the process.
He did not become angry or irritated as I expected and sincerely thanked
me and affirmed boldly that before the year ended, he was going to
be promoted. God told him that his promotion was his for the asking
and God never lies. I simply agreed with him on the latter point of his
statement and ended the meeting.

The next day, I met with his manage on another issue but could not end the conversation without discussing my meeting with Marcus. He confirmed that Marcus had pulled out the same manila folder and had the same conversation with him a few months ago. He said that he informed Marcus that he wasn't ready for a next-level position. He needed more experience under his belt to take on the added responsibilities of the new role. I left it at that.

Several weeks later while meeting with my boss, the CEO, she informed me that Marcus had met with her about his desire to be promoted. She said that Marcus told her the story of his career with the organization including all his accomplishments and achievements. I chuckled and informed her that he had the same conversation with me and with his manager. We both commented on Marcus' confidence and boldness but resigned to let his manager drive the issue.

Although I'm sure Marcus was disappointed by the outcome, his behavior nor his performance changed. In fact, his manager, the CEO, and I paid attention to Marcus now more than ever and were pleased with his engagement and performance even in the face of some disappointing news. A few days before Thanksgiving, Marcus' manager informed me that Marcus had submitted his resignation. He'd be leaving the organization after his four-week notice. His manger was very disappointed and was now ready to seriously consider a promotion for him. I worked with the manager to prepare the promotion offer and scheduled a meeting with Marcus to discuss.

When we offered Marcus the promotion, he thanked us for the consideration but respectfully declined. He recounted that he'd asked the organization three times and we refused. He really didn't want to, but he had no other recourse than to entertain opportunities outside of the organization. His new job came with a broader scope, the opportunity to direct his own team, a 25% increase in salary, and a bonus potential of up to 50% of his salary. His manager and I made several attempts to persuade him to stay, but he refused them all. He went on to tell us how the opportunity found him. He was working at Starbucks one evening and struck up a conversation with a woman who was sitting across from him at the table. He explained that God told him that he would be promoted before the end of the year. He divulged that he had asked us three times but each time, he was turned down. But he knew in his heart that someway it was going to happen because God told him that it would. He pulled out his manila folder and repeated his story to the woman at Starbucks. What Marcus didn't know was that the woman was the Chief Operating Officer (COO) at her company and had a management opening in the area akin to Marcus' profession. In the days that followed, the COO invited him in to meet the team and go through and a series of interviews. At the conclusion of his last interview, he was offered the new role, to which he accepted.

Marcus thanked us for listening to God and being a part of his plan to manifest what he had been promised. We lost a great employee but because of his boldness and Divine Audacity, he received what he wanted and what he was promised. Marcus never wavered, never lost faith, never threatened, never let his ego take over, never feared, and never settled for less in his quest to elevation. He moved in and by God and in doing so, God delivered. And it's interesting that the promotion was with another company. I love this part of the story because it shows us that God's vision for our lives is so much bigger, broader, and better than what we can sometimes ever imagine. God doesn't care about current employer, new employer, none of that. The request was for promotion and promotion with a different company was the good that God had just for Marcus.

I don't know where Marcus is today. I've looked for him on social media and through contacts with former colleagues, but no one knows where he is. I do know that his experience is ingrained in my consciousness as the model and example of the divine boldness that comes from trusting in God. I know for sure whether from Marcus' example or from the many demonstrations in my own experience that God wants us to move boldly and purposefully through our life experience, trusting and depending on Him. This is an output of choosing freedom over bondage.

The call to God is not complicated. We make a mistake of requiring peer approval for what we do. Peer approval requires the drawn-out pageantry to prove to others that your conviction and salvation are real. God does not require that at all. The desire to transform and belief in the power of God is all we need. Don't let the seeming appearance of peer approval or compliance to rituals deter you from your soul work. Turn within to God and begin your spiritual journey. It's never too late to start. It's never too late to start at the beginning or where you left off. Simply come to Him, believe in your heart and ye shall be saved. It's just that simple.

Think on These Things

1. After reading this chapter, how would you describe the "born again experience?"
2. What do you think Jesus meant when He said, "come unto me?" Who was he talking to?
3. Why is faith without works dead or non-existent? Explain.
4. What is the difference between audacity and "divine audacity?"
5. List five insights you gleaned from the Marcus story.

CHAPTER 5

The "Allness" of the I AM God

•●●●•

> *"There is one body and one Spirit, even as ye are called*
> *in one hope of your calling; one Lord, one faith one baptism,*
> *one God and Father of all, who is above all, and through all,*
> *and in you all,"(Ephesians 4:4-6 KJV).*

Reflecting on the Moses story from the last chapter, it has always been interesting to me that God referred to Himself as I Am. He didn't call Himself the master creator, or the King of Kings. He simply said, "I Am [all] that I Am." His message to Moses was that I AM all there is. I interpret this to mean God is whatever we need Him to be. If you are dealing with sickness or disease, I Am health. If you are having financial challenges, I Am wealth. If you are experiencing issues of sorrow and depression, I Am peace and stability of mind. I love it because it makes your relationship with God tailored and personal above reproach and opinion. No one can define God for you.

I catch myself using I Am statements negatively and immediately self-correct. This is especially true when I bump into someone on the train or in someone's way who's trying to walk past. "I'm sorry" seems to come out very easily. But this is a habit definitely worth breaking. I (Larry) am masterfully created in the image and likeness of God. Larry will never be sick, or broke, or sorry because my Father is not those things. I try not to speak them because I am aware of my inherited power to speak what I want and need into existence. When you say, I am sick, I am broke, I am worried, you attract those conditions into your experience. So, I am rich, I am healthy, I am prosperous – I am all the things I was created to be.

I have come to know for sure and am able to affirm that God is omniscient, omnipresent, and omnipotent. He is all. God is really not complicated when you understand his "allness" and our oneness with Him. The prefix "omni" is derived from the Latin root "omnis," which means all. Science means knowledge or knowing; present means widely or constantly encountered; potent means power. Simply stated, God is all knowledge, everywhere present and all the power that there is. Let's examine these more closely.

God Is Omniscient – ALL Knowledge Intelligence

God is not a smart God, or an intelligent God, or a God that knows a lot of stuff (adjectives). He Is intelligence (noun). He and all the knowledge and intelligence in the world are the same. Isaiah wrote, "Don't you yet understand? Don't you know by now that the everlasting God, the creator of the farthest parts of the earth, never grows faint or weary? No one can fathom the depths of his understanding," (Isaiah 40:28 The Living Bible TLB).

To understand God as omniscient is to understand Him as perfect knowledge of all things. We miss the awesomeness and greatness of God when we reduce Him or limit Him in consciousness. He is not like us (human). He doesn't have to learn a thing. He doesn't have to research, figure things out, hypothesize, or test any theory. He is not an experiential learner, nor does He learn from mistakes. He makes no mistakes. God does not discover or investigate. He knows all that has happened, all that's happening, and all happenings to come.

What does this mean for us?

We must learn how to tap into His omniscience. We are one with God, therefore, we have capacity to express to the highest degree our understanding of all that God is. Because God is omniscient, we don't have to know everything. We can tap into the omniscience of God for understanding, insight, and answers. In my role as a human resources leader, I have the authority to make decisions that impact the lives of many people. In making these decisions, especially those relative to hiring and firing, I gather all the information I can intellectually but often need to tap into the omniscience of God for guidance and confirmation. Success in whatever you do is already done using this omniscience.

The ability to tap into the omniscience will also qualify you for things you would not normally be qualified for. A couple of years ago, the HR function and the technology functions were combined in my organization. Overnight, I became the head of information technology and human resources. The first statement out of my mouth was, "I don't know a thing about running a technology function in an organization. What do I have to offer? Everyone who works for me will know more than I do." My boss explained that she needed a leader more than a technology expert. She expressed confidence in my ability to leverage the technical strengths of the technology team while providing vision, direction, and expectations in providing service to our staff. Since taking over IT, we have made tremendous progress in enabling the work of our employees, protecting our systems from external compromise, introducing new and relevant technology, and providing exceptional service to our customers. My leading through and with the omniscience of God has yielded great results for an area (under ordinary circumstances) I wouldn't be qualified to lead.

God, the omniscient will reveal to you answers to important questions in your consciousness to prevent you from worry and distress. David affirmed "the Lord will perfect that which concerns me; your mercy, O Lord, endures forever; do not forsake the works of your hands," (Psalms 138:8 NKJV). What concerns you concerns God. And because His will for you is complete and absolute good, He will not only answer your prayer, He'll give you abundantly, more than you asked. Our human side, guided primarily by our conscious phase of mind, will allow worry and stress to take over. Often, worry and stress show-up in your body as headaches, chest pains, elevated blood pressure and more. It is therefore of great importance that we trust God to provide what we need and are able to tap into his omniscience for answers to questions and concerns.

This will restore peace and order in our minds and bodies, which is the ideal state of being.

Earlier this year, my wife had a serious health challenge. What was initially diagnosed and treated as bronchitis quickly turned out to be something else. This challenge necessitated a hospital experience. The doctors tested her for everything, hoping to uncover the sources of her rigors, fever, respiratory issues and dip in blood pressure. Her results ruled out the common causes. Now it was time to test for the more serious stuff. This concerned us both. The medical professionals drew four huge vials of blood and admitted her to the hospital for what could have been three or four nights. I kept smiling, trying to keep her in positive and good spirits, but internally I was frightened and concerned. I prayed with her, kissed her goodnight and went home. When I got home, I prayed alone, affirming that the thing I was afraid of simply could not be. I pushed all thoughts of positive test results out of my mind. I went to bed and immediately fell into a sound sleep. It had been a long day. In the middle of the night, I woke up to close our bedroom windows as it was unseasonably cold for this time of year in the DC area. When I returned to bed, I felt intense heat on my face as if I were standing in the hot sun. I said aloud, "Father, what are you trying to tell me?" I went back to sleep. When I woke the next morning and sat on the side of the bed, I heard the Spirit say aloud, "it is well with my soul."

After I showered and got dressed, I called my wife to check on her. She told me that the doctors had been by and all her results came back negative and if she continued responding well to the antibiotics, she could go home the next day. We thanked God together but alone, I gave Him praises of thanksgiving for hearing my prayer, answering my prayer and allowing me to hear his intelligence speak directly to me regarding my wife's condition. I was operating in full and complete faith in God. When I arrived onto her floor, the nurses told me that they had just received the orders for her immediate discharge. I smiled and again thanked God. When I walked into the room she said, "guess what? I'm going home today." I responded that I knew and had packed her a change of clothes. She spent that night in her own bed and steadily over a few days grew in energy and strength. I know for sure that God is all knowledge-intelligence and He shares this knowledge/intelligence with me in providing absolute good in my life. Because of this dynamic, I've learned to trust more and fear less.

God Is Omnipresent – Equally Present in All Places

Although we refer to God as Father and use masculine pronouns (He, Him, His) in reference and reverence to God we forget that God is not a man. God is not a woman. God has no physical form. God is Spirit. He is present everywhere. And because He is everywhere present, we are always in his presence. He does not reside afar off in the sky. He's not in a robe, sitting in pious posture on a throne, looking down on us. He's not like an emergency response service, waiting to be dispatched from afar off to our rescue. God does not have to "show-up" nor "show-out." He is already there, here, everywhere. He is not limited by space. He is the everywhere present spirit of absolute good. Now that is good news and for some, new news!

David describes the phenomenon this way: "Where can I go from your Spirit? Or where can I flee from your presence? If I ascend into the heaven, you are there; if I make my bed in hell, behold you are there. If I take the wings of the morning and dwell in the uttermost parts of the sea, even there your hand shall lead me, and your right hand shall hold me. If I say surely the darkness will hide me and the light becomes night around me, even the darkness will not be dark to you. The night will shine like the day, for darkness is a light for you," (Psalms 139: 7-12 NKJV).

What does this mean for us?

This is certainly an aspect of God that has been made unnecessarily difficult. The idea that there is some secret path or process to access God is not true. The idea that if we face the East, or go to the lake, or go to our closet, we will find God, is simply incorrect. These are rituals, practices and folklore created and exercised over time without question or validation. The simple truth is that God is omnipresent, meaning he's everywhere present at the same time. And because He lives inside of us and outside of us everywhere, we are always in his presence. I live in Maryland. My friend Odell lives in Arkansas. Another friend Clay lives in Illinois. We (all three of us) are in the presence of God equally at the same time. That is amazing. That is a gift of grace and covering that makes God God.

I use the modifier "equally" for a reason. There is no more of God in one place than in the other. This is especially true on Sunday mornings. I remember asking a choir member if she wanted to come with me to visit another church after service. She said, "no, God ain't over there." Whether in the subdued Roman Catholic Church on the corner, or the bumping Baptist church in the middle of the block, or the charismatic and high-energy assembly in the suburbs, however expressed, there is no more God in one place than the other. Yes, it's a mystery. No, it cannot be rationalized, explained, or measured. Faith in God requires you to believe that the same God in the serpent-handling congregation down south is also in the same gender loving congregation up North. It's truth, it's principle whether you accept it or not.

Pursuant to your choice of freedom over bondage, access to the omnipresent always accessible-God is critical. Instant access to God is that connection and communion with God that blocks out the judgment and opinions of others, if you allow it. It's the special and private place where no one can hear the details of your conversation with God. And because he's omnipresent, and we are always in his presence, we have VIP private access to our own secret place.

Psalms 91 KJV speaks of this secret place. "He that dwelleth in the secret place of the most High shall abide under the shadow of the Almighty," (Psalms 91:1 KJV). When we use and rely on the Spirit of God within us and the Christ mind, our highest level of consciousness, we have access to the omnipresent God. And in His presence, there is no fear, no danger, no threat of harm. You can affirm with confidence that "… the Lord, He is my refuge and my fortress, my God, in Him will I trust," (Psalms 91:2 KJV). I'm excited about this refuge, this haven of peace, calmness, and safety. Dwelling in this place helps me build up the courage and fortitude I need to tackle the challenges that present themselves in my experience.

God Is Omnipotent – ALL the Power There Is

God is not powerful, nor should He be characterized and depicted as the most powerful God. God is ALL power. Power and God are one and the same. Another word for potent is able or ability, which means the capacity and capability to accomplish a goal or perform a task. God as "all able" or having "all ability" makes it clear that there is no inability or failure when it comes to God, as ability and power are God. Jesus said in speaking of His father and metaphysically of Himself, "…with man this is impossible but with God all things are possible," (Matthew 19:26 NIV).

What does this mean for us?

First it means that all other powers don't matter. Popular doctrine will compel you to believe in a duality of power in the universe. We declare with great conviction that God is omnipotent and is "all able" to do anything but then with equal conviction give energy to ideas of other powers. We have accepted and even practice the belief that God is in constant battle with the devil and his appointed ambassadors of evil. We subscribe to the powers of voodoo, witchcraft and other forms of evil-doing. We have become accepting and complacent with this constant threat to our spirit, mind, and body, the essence of who we are. It is sad and unfortunate that many believers cannot imagine their salvation or walk with God without the thought of the devil. When I began practicing in this new thought way, some close friends thought I had lost my mind. I was even told by one friend who is also a minister (we'll call him Reverend Mike) that to deny the existence and power of satan was a trick of satan himself (I refuse to capitalize the word satan). It was his opinion that the new thought people had "brain washed" me, and he was going to pray that I would make it back to God. I told Rev. Mike that I had not moved away from God. In fact and in truth, I had moved closer to God. I had moved away rather from thoughts and practices that emulate anything other than the only power there is in the world – God the good omnipotent.

I took Rev. Mike through a little exercise. I asked him if he believed that God was omnipotent-all power. He answered, "of course." I instructed him to make two fists. I then asked him a question: Imagine that God, all power, was in the right hand, what power was in his left? He responded, "the devil." I asked, how can that be possible? You just agreed with me that God was omnipotent – all power. If "all power" and "all ability" were in the right hand, how can any power be in the left? He responded, "I don't know, but what I do know is that the devil exists and it's my job through God to defeat him every day. Whether you believe it or not, we are in warfare with the devil." I told him that was a setup to fail. Keeping the devil at bay while daily working on your relationship with God was a bit much. I asked him to imagine his life daily focusing only on God; learning to hear His voice and emulating His characteristics and qualities and renewing his mind to be transformed. That, in itself, is a full-time job. Who has time to give energy to a non-existent, sub-spiritual power? The real work, I explained, was learning and growing powerful in operating in your highest self. The real work was learning how to clean-out all those negative and horrible thoughts stored in your subconscious phase of mind. The real work was embracing and practicing your divinity and expressing what it means to be a new creature. Paul makes it clear; "…If any man be in Christ, he is a new creature: old things are passed away; behold, all things are become new," (2 Corinthians 5:17 KJV). We agreed to disagree, but we haven't had the friendship we used to have since that conversation. Now I fully understand Paul's question in his letter to the folks in Galatia, "Am I therefore become your enemy because I tell you the truth?" (Galatians 4:16 KJV). Old things, those thoughts, beliefs, and feelings we blithely subscribe to that yield no results or demonstrations, they are gone. All things are new. The way I look at my world is refreshed, renewed, and brand new. Why, because I am a new creature.

I love Mike (present tense) and I miss his company and friendship. He was the friend that could always make me laugh when I really didn't feel like laughing. We were truly "hommies." But although we were hommies, and although I still love him, my spiritual freedom is priceless, and I cannot compromise my truth. As the older Christians would say, I leave him lovingly in the hands and care of God. I continue to affirm that there is no duality of power in the universe. The only power, the only presence that exists is God, the omnipotent; the everywhere present and benevolent Spirit intelligence. There can be nothing else.

Secondly, God as omnipotent gives us a level of supernatural confidence and assurance some do not have. The believer and practitioner of this truth is aware that he can tap into God's omnipotence to accomplish or achieve any goal or desire of his heart that's to his highest good. In one of Paul's letters to the Philippians, he affirms, "I can do all things through Him who gives me strength," (Philippians 4:13 NIV). We act in error when we make statements of doubt about our abilities and possibilities. I did this often. "I can't be a VP; I can't afford a new house; I can't pass that certification exam." When we begin a statement with "I can't," what we're really saying is that not only do I doubt my ability to achieve or accomplish, I doubt that even I AM can. This is a mistake. The truth is that if you really wanted to, you could have, own, possess, attain, and acquire anything to your highest good because nothing is impossible for the omnipotent God. I think this empowering message of truth scares people. There is an unhealthy and irrational level of comfort in not doing all you can do to live a better life. "I'm just waiting on the Lord," means I'm not going to put forth any energy to build my consciousness and prepare myself to receive. As someone who operated this way, I know for sure that when it comes to my salvation, there is never a time for complacency. Yes, I take my burdens to the Lord and leave them there, but I am reading, praying, affirming and doing the work to attract more good and fewer occurrences that end up as burdens.

Thirdly, understanding God as omnipotent helps us to define God for ourselves. I've discovered that my spiritual work is personal. What I believe and how I practice what I believe does not require clearance or approval from anyone. There is no need to argue, justify or persuade others to be "OK" with what I believe. I posit that every believer has to define who and what God is for themselves.

In defining Him personally, it is important not to limit God in any way. One of the greatest sermons I've ever heard was delivered by the Reverend Dr. Johnnie Colemon entitled, *How Big is Your God?"* In this sermon, she challenged the congregation to stop limiting God to what you think will probably happen. Before I really understood that all things are possible with the omnipotent God, I used to pray and ask for what I thought I'd probably get. But now I trust the "bigness" of God "who is able to do exceedingly abundantly above all that we ask or think according to the power that worketh in us," (Ephesians 3:20 KJV). God is as able and capable as your awareness. The limits and boundaries you've created in your mind about God are illusions. The human side of you loves the "assumed safety" of boundaries and limits. The spiritual part of you understands that relative to God, there are no boundaries and no limits.

I read a summary of an interesting experiment/study relative to how our minds embrace boundaries. A team of landscape architects conducted a study to observe the psychological influences of having a fence around a playground, and how its consequent effects would impact preschool children. By observing teachers and their students on a playground with no fence, the researchers found a striking difference in how the children interacted in the space.

On playgrounds without fences, the children tended to gather around the teacher and were reluctant to stray far from her view. On playgrounds that were fenced, however, they ran all around the entire playground, feeling free to explore and tended to play closer to the fence. The researchers concluded that with a boundary (in this case a fence) the children felt more at ease to explore the space.

What was interesting to me about this study was on the playground without a fence, the children kept close to the teacher. This suggests that somewhere early in our psychological development, we associated the idea of safety with boundaries, to the point of creating them where they don't exist. You would think that the children would run free, happy that they were able to do so, knowing that they were being monitored from afar. But no child ran free. So it is with some people relative to the idea of God as omnipotent. There is a tendency to stay close to the old and familiar ideas and beliefs about God. Some things are just "too big" for God. For some it means safety and protection from disappointment and the critique of others. Running free or playing far from the teacher would be silly and dangerous. But God wants us to run free. He does not want us to settle for what we perceive to be safe and a sure thing. He wants us to cancel all the thoughts and beliefs that are active in the crevasses of our subconscious that limit His capability and capacity. He wants us to build the consciousness for the big things. He wants us to not let boundaries, physical or mental, hold us stagnant. He wants you to reach for a mansion over a townhouse. He wants you to reach for good health and not just one day at a time (sweet Jesus). We have unfortunately allowed fear and disappointment to make us forget the power that God has to provide any and everything we want and need. "Fear not little flock; for it is your Father's good pleasure to give you the kingdom," (Luke 12:32 KJV). And what could be better than living in a manner that gives God pleasure? It's time to repent (change your mind) and live a life with a consciousness of "limitlessness" instead of limitation.

Lastly, understanding God as omnipotent with access to this power anytime and anywhere, teaches us the importance and power of our imagination. I get excited when I think about, talk about and write about the power of imagination. I'm already thinking about a book focused solely on the power of imagination. Albert Einstein, one of the greatest physicist and scientific minds of our time once said, "Imagination is better than intelligence." Knowing what I know for sure about imagination, I agree with his opinion wholeheartedly. Intelligence describes the ability to understand facts about what already exists. Imagination describes our ability to form images about things that do not yet exist. In Paul's letter to the people of Rome, he submits, "…I have made you a father of many nations in the presence of Him who he believed – God, who gives life to the dead and calls those things which do not exist as though they did," (Romans 4:17 NKJV). Our power of imagination is very important to our pursuit of a happy, healthy and prosperous life. It's through this imaging that we make specific our request to God. Then, we allow the Divine Strategy to be activated, bringing our wants, needs, and desires to fruition.

Reflecting back on the twelve powers introduced by Charles Fillmore, I understand and work with them as the qualities and attributes of God. Imagination is one of the most important powers we have as spiritual beings. Mainstream doctrine and teachings are dismissive of these powers including imagination. This is partly due to varied definitions of their meanings. Some, reading this book are considering imagination as a spiritual power for the first time. That's great because there is less to unlearn.

The intellectual definition of imagination is "the faculty or action of forming new ideas or images or concepts of external objects not present in the senses." Spiritually, I define imagination as the "big screen" in my mind that shows the ideas and images and concepts of "what can be." No other living creation has the power to see something that does not exist or "what can be." Because we are masterfully created in the image and likeness of God the omnipotent, we have the ability to form images of our "highest good" desires and then the power to speak them into existence. God Himself demonstrated this power when He created the universe. Even in his omniscience and omnipotence, God had an image of what He wanted to create and then spoke it into existence. God's first words were "let there be," which brought forth the creation of the universe including man.

You and I have the same ability. Because everything begins in mind, your ability to build, design and establish your heart's desire is not trivial or futile. Those internally developed images serve as prayers, which say to the universe "let it be for me." God is done creating. He's not creating more planets, mountains, or bodies of water. Likewise He does not create houses, cars or cash. When you carve out and make room for these things on your mind's big screen and then speak them into your experience, the universe and all herein "click" into play to bring them to you. Think about a safe. When you know the combination and use the dial to enter it, the inner wheels and mechanisms work to open the door. That's what happens here. Your formed images and your prayers create this universal working of people, circumstances, and opportunities to bring your imagined state into existence. Some call it coincidence, or luck, or your season. As a spiritual being, I don't necessarily believe in coincidence, or luck or seasons of blessings. I call this Divine Strategy. When God compels the universe and the people herein to click into action on my behalf, decisions are made, access is granted, and information is provided toward manifestation. The late Reverend Olivia Jones who was a prophet and my pastor at one point used to say, "…and if God is in a hurry, he'll take an angel, put some skin and clothes on him, and send him down to deliver your blessing to your front door. People will come into your life situation to help you and then you'll never see or hear from them again. That's an angel."

When Ramona and I found our first home, we opted to rent it with an option to purchase later. We wanted to make sure that the house and the area was where we wanted to be long-term. After a couple of years, we decided to purchase, so we began looking at finance options. Although our credit had improved, securing financing for a house was not easy. We pursued traditional and a few non-traditional options to no avail. One day at the barbershop while discussing the challenge with my barber Jeff, Calvin walked in. Jeff suggested that I speak with Calvin because he was involved in real estate. I was not enthusiastic about speaking with yet another broker just to be denied or discouraged. But Jeff was uncharacteristically insistent that I connect with Calvin and immediately introduced us. To my surprise, Calvin was a cool guy. He was bit eccentric but was genuinely positive and excited to help us. Do you hear the clicks?

Over the course of the next few weeks, Ramona and I met with Calvin several times, completed the necessary paperwork and submitted our application to the mortgage company. Understanding that we were not Calvin's only client, we were patient when we couldn't connect with him. This was before the age of the Internet, so everything was done on paper and by telephone. When we did hear from Calvin, he did not have good news to share. We were bummed but Calvin was very positive. He was determined to find a solution for us. He was successful. We were finally approved and set for closing. Calvin showed up for the closing but strangely enough, after ten minutes later, his car was being towed. He left the closing and that was the last time we saw or heard from him. Even after we closed and began settling in as homeowners, no Calvin. I tried contacting him and inquiring about him at the barbershop. Jeff's experience and mine were similar. Calvin had disappeared.

I know for sure that it was no coincidence that Calvin and I were in the barbershop at the same time on the same day. Nor was it luck that Calvin had knowledge and experience with various financing options.

I know for sure that Calvin was a part of God's Divine Strategy to bless us with what we needed to become homeowners. We saw ourselves being approved for financing. We imagined ourselves painting the walls, upgrading the kitchen, and entertaining in our home, and praise God, the universe clicked into action to bring us what we envisioned and imagined. So was Calvin an angel? Maybe we'll never know, but what we know for sure is that he was a part of the strategy to facilitate our image of home. So let them call you weird or a dreamer. It's okay because "where there is no vision, the people will parish...," (Proverbs 29:18 KJV). Don't go to sleep on your God-given, potent, and effective power of imagination. Watch God work. "Now watch as the Lord does great miracles," (1 Samuel 12:16 The Living Bible TLB).

Think on These Things

1. What does it mean to us that God is omnipresent, omniscient, and omnipotent?
2. What lesson did you personally glean from the playground experiment?
3. Do you agree with Einstein? How is imagination greater than intelligence? Explain.
4. Think of four to five "I am" statements you erroneously speak. Write the replacement statement for them below.

CHAPTER 6

The Imperatives for Better Living

• • ● • •

> "If I shut up the heavens so that there is no rain, or if I
> command the locust to devour the land, or if I send pestilence
> among my people, and my people who are called by my name,
> humble themselves, and pray, and seek my face, and turn
> from their wicked ways, then I will hear from heaven, forgive
> their sins and will heal the land. Now my eyes will be open
> and my ears attentive to take prayer offered in this place. For
> now, I have chosen and consecrated this house that my name
> may be there forever, and my eyes and my heart will be there
> perpetually," (2 Chronicles 7:13-16 KJV).

A scholar of the bible would not describe Chronicles as an exciting biblical
work. In fact, it's assumed that most people flip right past Chronicles to
find more animated or action-oriented reading. That said, we should
not "go to sleep" on Chronicles as it provides one of the most profound
messages of divine favor in the old testament. The anonymous author
(also known as the Chronicler) does more than provide detail of the
rich genealogy of the ancient Israelites, he makes a new presentation
of old material that provides a message of hope. The Bible Project, an
independent source of bible research describes the Chronicler's work
as more than just "cool theology." "The book's message has a pastoral
purpose: to bring comfort and hope to generations of God's people who
were tempted towards despair or apathy. During a time when many

wondered if God was ever going to fulfill his promises, the Chronicler retold the story of their collective past in order to rekindle hope for the future," (Not Just, 4).

At the dedication of the temple built to primarily house the Ark, Solomon participated in the service to remind people not to give up on God and to stand on his promises. Even if the heavens were to withhold rain, or the locust attacked, or pestilence was released among the people, Solomon's message was clear: humble yourself, pray, seek God's face, and turn away from your wicked thoughts, words and ways, then God would heal and deliver. I think of them as imperatives (i.e. essential, urgent, of vital importance) of better living. Although the label sounds a bit grander than I intended, I submit that Christians (His people who were called by His name) must be able to practice these basic imperatives to live in the way that God intends: free, healthy, prosperous, and wealthy. Let's examine these imperative in more detail.

The Humility Imperative

> *"So humble yourselves under the mighty power of God and at the right time, He will lift you up in honor," (1 Peter 5:6 New Living Translation NLT).*

At the onset, we need to have one working definition of humility. The definition I like is "total dependence on God." As such, it cannot mean weakness or self-hatred. It speaks to the very core essence of our relations with the Father. Ego, arrogance, and superiority are polarities of humility that put us out of spiritual order. Any state of consciousness we are in where we put ourselves above or in front of God is an error.

As children and followers of God, through Him and only through Him, are we able to do great and sustaining things for ourselves and others. Through His omniscience, we are able to envision, build, create, and invent products and services with the potential to positively impact the lives of millions of people. These million-dollar ideas help create wealth and prosperity, which are the promises of God. Should we be proud of our discoveries and accomplishments? Of course we should.

Pride belongs to us, and we belong to it because it is who we are. Pride is at the core of our very nature. But it's pride of what we've achieved through God, putting Him first, giving Him credit and reverence for all He has enabled us to accomplish.

God does not require us to think of ourselves as nothings. I grew-up thinking that I was a worm of the dust, a speck in God's eye, and a filthy rag. I was taught that I was not important to God and if I was not important to Him, surely, I couldn't be important to anyone else. These so-called teachings all came under the banner of humility. I have since repented (changed my mind) and rejected these teachings because they are false. I am extremely important to God. I'm His greatest creation. There is no other living creature that is designed to do the things God designed me to do. I am masterfully made in his image and likeness. That's why I am afforded his amazing grace, mercy, love, and favor. That's why it pleases Him when I spend my time thinking and acting upon ways to express Him in all I think, say and do. Humility is not thinking less of yourself. Humility is thinking of yourself less and God more. I fill my mind full of good and wonderful stuff with God smack dab in the middle. Thinking of his omnipotence and omniscience gives me confidence that I can make good decisions, come up with solutions to my challenges and help others through Him working in and through me. This is what Paul meant when he wrote, "Finally brethren, whatsoever things are true, whatsoever things are honest, whatsoever things are just, whatsoever things are pure; whatsoever things are lovely, whatsoever things are of good report, if there be any virtue and if there be any praise, think on these things," (Philippians 4:8 KJV). I fill my mind with ideas and the possibilities of greatness and loveliness as I am led and directed by the Christ Spirit within.

There are many ways to express humility and it's up to us (based on our personal level of understanding) to determine how we will individually express. I offer the following as a starting point.

Service

Jesus Christ, our Wayshower, demonstrated and provided one of the greatest examples of humility as a servant to his disciples. During the meal before the Passover Festival, He stood, removed His clothing and wrapped a towel around His waist. One by one, He began washing the feet of the disciples. A critical lesson followed. "When He had finished washing their feet, He put on His clothes and returned to his place. Do you understand what I have done for you? He asked them. You call me 'teacher' and 'Lord' and rightly so, for that is what I am. Now that I, your Lord and Teacher, have washed your feet, you also should wash one another's feet. I have set you an example that you should do as I have done for you," (John 13:12-14 NIV).

In those days, foot washing was a common practice in every home. People wore sandals or were often bare foot. The roads were always dusty and dirty from garbage and even animal waste in the streets. It was pretty disgusting to sit around during and after a meal enduring the smell and site of dirty feet, so as a gesture, hosts would command house servants to wash the feet of the guests. Usually the lowest servant of the household was expected to wash the feet of the guests. Because Jesus and the disciples were in a private-home without servants, Jesus took it upon Himself to serve in this capacity.

I believe Jesus washed the feet of the disciples to demonstrate what it looked like to serve and be humble. He lowered Himself physically and in consciousness to the level of the lowest servant to serve the disciples. The lesson here is that when we lower ourselves to serve, we exalt God. We are in order and behaving in a manner that pleases God. We acknowledge that every human being is seen as equal in His sight. That's why it's so important to treat people with dignity and respect regardless of their race, gender, sexual orientation, religious beliefs and all the other labels you can think of. Lowering the "highest of yourself" to the level of equality (as God sees us) and serving your fellow brother or sister is paramount to what it means to be "called by his name."

Service to others means that you take your talents, knowledge, skills and abilities and use them to help those who would benefit from them.

Whether you're a member of the usher board, lead singer in the choir, community volunteer, or member of the PTA, you are operating in obedience to God. And it makes no sense to serve begrudgingly or angry or out of guilt and obligation. Your negative disposition to service is empty and impotent. "The point is this: whosoever sows sparingly will also reap sparingly; and whosoever sows bountifully will also reap bountifully. Each one must give as he has decided in his heart, not reluctantly or under compulsion, for God loves a cheerful giver," (2 Corinthians 9:6-7 English Standard Version ESV). Most only think about money when reading or reflecting on this scripture, but I think it is also germane to the giving of our talents and time to others for our and their higher good.

Acknowledgment

"Trust in the Lord with all your heart and lean not on your own understanding; in all your ways acknowledge Him, and He shall direct your paths," (Proverbs 3: 5-6 NKJV). Because God is omnipresent, we are always in His presence. He is everywhere evenly present to advise, warn, and lead us in a manner that is both correct and good. When we lower ourselves (our own understanding) and acknowledge (recognize) His power and perfect will for us, we make the right choices, walk the right path, and avoid harm. Sounds simple right? But in practice, it's not that simple. We take pride in thinking independently and for ourselves. When confronted with a challenge, we rise up in human understanding, dictating our actions forward. In doing so, we miss the privilege and benefit of God's guidance and will for us. Not with just the big things but all things (all your ways). We express humility by trusting in God and choosing His will and way over our own. Again, it sounds simple, but it requires practice.

Years ago, I changed jobs and organizations. On the Thursday of my first week on the new job, I began receiving phone calls from friends and former colleagues. One of the ladies (we'll call her Joyce) was making some very disparaging remarks about me and my performance. As I recall, Joyce and I really didn't have the best relationship while I was there. It was her opinion that in my role as HR manager, I should be working harder for the Black employees than the White employees in hiring, promoting and remuneration. In the past, I have politely informed her that her opinions were erroneous and discriminatory. So I was not surprised that she had a negative opinion of me but certainly not to the point where she would actively defame my character especially since I was no longer there. I was angry and had an immediate desire to "cuss her out" and vindicate myself. I made a decision to get Joyce straight and in person. I called my new supervisor and told her I had an emergency and would be late to work the next day. On Friday morning I dressed to impress and headed to the old office with the energetic intent to "lay Joyce flat," not with my fists but with my words.

In the elevator on the way up, I prayed in error. I actually asked God to help me get through the confrontation without getting emotional or belligerent (I had somewhat of a temper in those days). At that moment, I heard the voice of the late Reverend Clarence Cobbs say, "it makes no difference what you think of me, but it does make a difference what I think of you." Reverend Cobbs was the founder and pastor of the First Church of Deliverance in Chicago and one of the greatest prophets of our time. I remember staying up late on Sunday nights to hear him and the church's 11:00 p.m. broadcast. At the halfway point before the sermon and with the choir bumping in the background, he would affirm this truth. He reminded listeners that they would not be judged by what others thought of them, rather by what they thought of others. Even in my error praying, I acknowledged the presence of God, and He re-directed my path. I decided at that moment that Joyce's opinions of me didn't matter. I knew her assertions were not true and decided to ignore her opinions and words. I also decided to tell the "messengers" that I didn't want to hear it, because it is not what she thinks but what I think that make it so. I spent my time at the office visiting with my friends and enjoying their company. When I ran into Joyce, I was flowing so strong in peace, I spoke to here before I knew it. I just couldn't help myself. I lowered myself (my own understanding) and allowed myself to be led by the Christ Spirit within me. In that instance, order was regained within. In that instance, Joyce and her disparaging comments lost their potency and importance, and the need to be vindicated disappeared. We express humility by aligning our actions to His will – not our own.

Thankfulness

"Every good and perfect gift is from above, coming down from the Father of the heavenly lights, who does not change like shifting shadows," (James 1:17 NIV). All ideas, discoveries and illuminations come from God through our Christ mind. As we discussed in chapter three, that's the part of your mind that is constantly in tune with the Spirit of the Christ. And to that end, can bring nothing but good. When we receive these good ideas, discoveries and illumination it is incumbent upon us to attribute them, not to self but to the source – God the omniscient. We express humility in thanking God for what we've received. The big things, medium things and small things, it pleases God when we thank Him and give Him credit for His good. In Paul's letter to the church in Thessalonica, he compels them to "give thanks in all circumstances; for this is God's will for you in Christ Jesus," (1 Thessalonians 5:18 NIV).

Attributing and giving thanks to God for your good helps to reinforce your trust and dependence upon Him. It's comparable to exercising a muscle in your body. The more you flex and stretch and move, the stronger and firmer it becomes. You will begin to receive more ideas and your demonstrations will evolve to be bigger and bolder. As you practice the presence of God, fear and trepidation will dissipate. Your reliance on others will be replaced with a reliance on God. You will begin to flow in the limitlessness of God, relying on his guidance and instruction. In attributing your good to God and having a spirit of thanksgiving, you will become a powerful new creature in Christ Jesus.

The Prayer Imperative

"... And He spoke a parable unto them to this end, that man ought always pray and not faint," (Luke 18:1 KJV).

The disciples asked Jesus to teach them one thing: how to pray. They witnessed time after time Jesus speaking aloud and withdrawing into silence and meditation in communication with his Father – His God self. And after He prayed, miracles happened. The dead walked alive, the adulteress was exonerated, and a hungry multitude was fed. To the disciples, there was something to this prayer thing, and they knew that in order to live the righteous and free life they were called to lead, it was imperative that they learned how to pray.

Of all the things we need to learn as believers, praying is the easiest. If you are like me, you were raised with a belief that not everyone could "get a prayer through." Everyone didn't know how to pray. I now know that those teachings are completely erroneous. There is no such thing as "getting a prayer though." If so, I ask through what? We've learned that we are always in the presence of God. There is nothing to get through in connecting and communing with the Father. There is no barrier or "middle man" needed to connect to the Christ Spirit that is within all of us. Because we are masterfully made, we are always connected to the Father, who hears every single prayer we pray.

So what is prayer (good place to start)? What does it mean to pray? Here is the definition I like: Prayer is communing with (talking and listening to) God. Not a complicated imperative at all. When you still yourself and address God, you have his undivided attention. All you have to do is speak as if you were speaking to a friend or loved one. There's no special place, preferred direction, or specific posture. Your head does have to be bowed nor your eyes closed. Your words don't have to rhyme or be latent with a series of chosen scriptures or biblical references. After getting His attention by calling His name (I use Father God), begin to express as you are led in and by Spirit. I wish I could tell you that I've discovered some secret or offer some guarantee – I can't. No one can. Prayer is personal and above all the criticism and opinions of others.

Here are a few things I've discovered about prayer:

I Enjoy Praying

As children, prayer was positioned as a chore. At night, we were directed to do our homework, take a bath, brush our teeth, and say our prayers. Unfortunately for some, prayer remains a chore or what you do when you really want something. Prayer went from being our proverbial steering wheel to be our spare tire. Let's change our mindset about praying right here and now. It is an honor and opportunity to talk to God. He, the Christ within, wants to hear from us. "For the eyes of the Lord are on the righteous and his ears are attentive to their prayer…" (1 Peter 3:12 NIV). But what if I'm not righteous? Is it a waste of time to pray if I'm not living the way I should live, have sinned, or even backslidden? The answer is absolutely not!

Righteousness is not a destination or final state of completion, rather it's a journey. Being "right" is not a one and done or level that's attained and then disregarded. Daily, hourly, by the minute, we all are in some form of "rightness," striving to be more right than wrong. You are in a state of "rightness" when you have a mind or spirit to talk to God.

I've learned to enjoy talking to God because the act relieves me, comforts me, and calms me. I feel better about my challenges when I pray. And when I'm fearful, talking to God makes me feel protected and comforted. And when I'm attuned to His presence, He speaks to me. Yes, the Lord speaks, and He will speak to you either through the still small voice, signs and wonders, or through the manifestation of the seemingly impossible. "Give me a sign of your goodness, that my enemies may see it and be put to shame, for you Lord, have helped me and comforted me," (Psalms 86:17 NIV). Ideas will come. Instructions will come. Answers will come. People (some you've never met before) will come to you and help you. Some will even say, "I don't know why I'm doing this, but I feel compelled to help you." This is a sign that God has heard and is answering your prayers. One of the greatest feelings in the world is when you pray, and the Holy Spirit comes forth and brings calm and peace to your body and mind. You may not dance as David did or speak in tongues like the disciples in the upper room, but you will express in a manner that is genuine and personal as led by Spirit.

Exercise Dominion

"Then God said, let us make man in our image, after our likeness. And let them have dominion over the fish of the sea, and over the birds of the heavens and over the livestock and over the earth and over every creeping thing that creeps on the earth," (Genesis 1:26 KJV).

To have dominion means that I am in charge. I rule over it and have authority to do with it as I will. God gave me dominion over everything in my experience: what's already here and what's to come. The significance of Genesis 1:26 is less about the fish, birds and livestock (the tangible) and more about the gifts of God (the intangible). I have jurisdiction and rights to control what God has given me to control. I use my authority and dominion through kinship to God to call the things I need and want into existence.

In this awareness of dominion, I've learned to use fewer nouns and more verbs when I pray. When the Father created the heavens and earth, He did so through a series of prayers which displayed his dominion and authority. Each prayer began with Let There Be! Through His commanding authority, He created the heavens, earth, light, land, vegetation, stars, creeping things, and man. Is it so hard to imagine that we, created in his image and likeness and with limitless dominion, cannot do the same thing? No, we are not going to create another planet or more oceans and mountains. We can, however, command wealth, good relationships, health, material desires of our hearts, and all things to our highest good into existence.

Growing up in the church, I now understand why prayer is an imperative that many find too difficult to learn. The deacons and ministers pray so eloquently and effortlessly to where we can't imagine ourselves ever expressing at that level. I think of Deacon Frank Quinn, who I called uncle Frank, and Deacon Leslie Sanders, Sr., Deacon Mack Connor, and my dad who could set the church on fire with their powerful and charismatic prayers. But I submit that imitation or duplication of "assembly prayer" is not necessary and certainly not the model. All that's required is your authentic self and a foundation of faith. Faith, knowing and expecting God to answer your prayer, is demonstrated when we use more verbs than nouns. We don't need to send God anywhere. We don't have to tell Him to go by the hospital or send Him to our jobs. We don't need to instruct Him to come through the classroom or visit a church mother in the nursing home. He is omnipresent – he's already everywhere. Exercise your dominion and faith with action words and phrases. Consider these prayers: Father:

- Let there be wealth and prosperity in my life.
- Bring peace, collaboration and fairness to my work life. Equip me with the knowledge, skills and abilities I need to perform my work above and beyond the expectation of my appraisers.
- Move in my body. Free my body of all alignments, pain, and disease.
- Protect and cover me as I travel throughout the day and in my home.
- Sustain love, honor, and respect to my marriage and all my relationships.
- Deliver me from all thoughts of lack, loss, and inferiority.
- Raise and uphold my consciousness to know, trust, and practice your omniscience, omnipresence and omnipotence.

All the aforementioned are prayers. They are powerful and effective and serve as the conduit to all that we need. "…the effective fervent prayer of a righteous man avails much," (James 5:16 NKJV).

Not to Worry

I once heard a minster say, if you're going to worry, don't pray and if you're going to pray, don't worry. Paul advised, "do not be anxious about anything, but in everything by prayer and supplication with thanksgiving, let your requests be made known to God. And the peace of God, which surpasses all understanding, will guard your hearts and your minds in Christ Jesus," (Philippians 4:6-7 ESV). The Merriam-Webster

Dictionary defines "anxiety" as "apprehensive uneasiness or nervousness, usually over an impending or anticipated ill." Anxiety shows up in our bodies as accelerated heart rates, rapid breathing, sweating, and tiredness or exhaustion. Anxiety has also been linked to other serious health conditions such as ulcers, debilitating headaches, and heart disease.

Here is some good news – anxiety and worry does not change who God is. Remember, He's not a god. He's God the good omnipotent. His essence is absolute good. All the good we see, experience, and pursue is an output or out pouring of God. If you ask God for something to your highest good, the universe, through God, is working to bring it to you, whether you worry or not. God does not punish you for worrying. But it's important to understand that worry is more about you and less about God. Here is a very important question: why allow anxiety and stress into your consciousness? Why allow this thing to pull you out of faith, freedom, and peace and into doubt, worry, and strife? God is going to do it! It's not necessary to harm ourselves with these thoughts. Put your trust in God. Stay in the God consciousness. Push these files from your subconscious phase of mind down and away from you.

I learned how to worry at an early age, and I have no one to blame for this but myself. I'm an action-oriented person. It was hard for me to turn it over to the Lord. Doing all I could do and then turning it over to the Lord felt like I was not working on it. I felt lazy and defeated. In my prior level of awareness, worrying gave me energy. I was "all in" on solving the problem myself. Praise God, I have abandoned that old thinking. I breathe, relax, and calm myself in the blessed assurance that God's gonna keep his promise. And once you let go, fulfillment is swift, full, and complete.

I remember working on a job I didn't like. I went from having a boss I adored, trusted and respected to one that led through fear and intimidation. Knowing that it was time to go, I began a job search. I remember this job search being a bit more challenging because I was being very selective, not wanting to jump out of the proverbial skillet into the frying pan. Inquiry after inquiry and interview after interview, I could not find an employer that I wanted to partner with. I was growing extremely weary and decided to just endure the pain of my current employment situation. I needed to take a break and pick up my search again in a few months. I had one more interview that I almost forgot about. It was with a professional association headquartered in a Chicago suburb not too far from where I lived. I had the idea of canceling but the Spirit within instructed me to follow-through on my commitment. I remember praying in the elevator for God to help me speak and present myself as the best candidate for this job but if it was going to be old wine in new skins, I didn't want it. It turned out to be a great opportunity with a great organization and a great manager who I fell in love with in that first meeting (which went an hour over the allotted time scheduled). It was only the first interview but afterwards, I told God that this was the job I wanted. I prayed for an offer. About a week later, I was asked back for a second interview. I showed-up with my PowerPoint presentation that illustrated and outlined my vision for managing talent in this organization. I met all the key leaders including the CEO.

After the final interview, we began our drive to Orlando for a family vacation. I was told that I'd be contacted the following week, the week of my vacation. I wrote my thank you letters, called to check on the status and everything else I could to move things along. I was done doing all I could do, so I decided to worry. I realized that my worrying was having a negative influence on our vacation, so I decided to let it go until we returned home. Another week had passed, we were now back home and still no word – no offer. I was a wreck for three days, checking my voicemail and email incessantly. The following Monday morning on my way to work, I released it. I decided to let go and let God. I had done all I could and knew what God had for me was for me. On Tuesday morning, my former boss who I listed as a reference called to inform me that she had received a call from the company. She said she gave me a "glowing" reference. This was a great sign, and I was again hopeful. I wanted to do something and worrying again was certainly an option. This time, however, I decided to go on my way and not worry, trusting and believing that what God had for me was for me. Ten minutes after my decision not to resume worrying and let God work it out, I received a phone call with an apology for taking so long and an offer of employment. We chatted, I gladly accepted, discussed a start date and ended the call.

When I hung up, I dropped to my knees and thanked God for this good He had bestowed on me, my life and the quality of life for my family.

Worrying didn't stop God from blessing me but when I looked back at all the unnecessary worrying and anxiety, it added absolutely no value to the situation and was a colossal waste of time. My anxiety only resulted in over-eating, not sleeping, and being emotionally absent from my family and staff. When I put my full trust in God and let it go, my good was released. I share this lesson of choosing prayer over anxiety and worry as one of my greatest lessons and another milestone on my spiritual journey.

Seek My Face – The "Followership" Imperative

"When Jesus spoke again to the people, he said, I am the light of the world. Whoever follows me will never walk in darkness but will have the light of life," (John 8:12 NIV).

The Wayshower never asked or required us to praise Him, nor worship Him, nor bow before Him. His only command to us was to follow Him. I call it "followership." Followership becomes a critical imperative because it prescribes how we should live, move and have our being. It also prescribes how we engage with other believers and non-believers in this experience. In Hebrew, the word face is translated as "presence." If God is omnipresent and as a result, we are always in his presence, what does it mean to seek his presence?

I believe we seek his presence when we express or emulate his ways. Jesus is referred to as the Wayshower for a very good reason: His life was the model for us to live. Years ago, the slogan "what would Jesus do" was very popular inside and outside of religious circles, and it really sums up this imperative very well. We seek his face when we choose to pattern our lives as he demonstrated while on earth. I think it is useless to learn these practices and embrace these new thoughts and ideas about God and keep them to ourselves. How we live and how we relate to others should be an authentic and consistent demonstration of our followership of the Christ within. These are the things I've learned in demonstrating followership.

"Up" Your Thinking

"Let this mind be in you which was also in Christ Jesus,"
(Philippians 2:5 KJV).

Grammatically, the word up is an adverb or a preposition, depending on its exact use. I am using my editorial freedom to change it into a verb within this context. Earlier in the book, we learned about the three phases of mind: Christ consciousness (mind), consciousness, and the subconscious phase of mind. As you will recall, the highest level of consciousness is also referred to as the Christ mind. It is always in tune with the Christ spirit within you and communicates through guidance, warnings, and ideas in your best interest and for your highest good. Thinking, the movement of ideas in the mind, is how we appraise and decide how to act and respond to these thoughts.

We seek His face or practice his presence when we align our thoughts, decisions, actions, and reactions to the Christ mind. We emulate and demonstrate the qualities and attributes of God when we make choices imparted to us from Spirit through our Christ mind. This is how the Wayshower modeled living for us. His decisions and actions were in line with those of His Father. You have never read in the bible about Jesus worrying, making a mistake, having regret, over-spending, feeling abandoned, or having to give someone a piece of his mind. It is because he "up-ed" his thinking. He dwelt in the secret place, that high chamber of thinking we all have. He abided in the shadow or covering of God. He did not lower his thinking by relying on what he heard, felt, or saw through his conscious or subconscious phases of mind. He "up-ed" His thinking to the highest level.

I love the story captured by Matthew about the temptation of Jesus by the tempter (metaphysically, His lowest state of consciousness). It's a great demonstration from the Wayshower of what it means to "up" your thinking. "Then Jesus was led by the Spirit into the wilderness to be tempted by the devil. After fasting 40 days and 40 nights, He was hungry. The tempter came to Him and said, if you are the Son of God, tell these stones to become bread. Jesus answered, 'it is written. Man shall not live on bread alone, but on every word that comes from the mouth of God.' Then the devil took Him to the holy city and had Him stand on the highest point of the temple. If you are the Son of God, he said, throw yourself down. For it is written, He will command his angels concerning you and they will lift you up in their hands so that you will not strike your foot against a stone. Jesus answered him, 'it is also written, do not put the Lord your God to the test.' Again the devil took Him to a very high mountain and showed Him all the kingdoms of the world and their splendor. All this I will give you, he said, if you will bow down and worship me. Jesus said to him, 'away from me satan. For it is written, worship the Lord your God and serve Him only.' Then the devil left Him, and angels came and attended Him," (Matthew 4:1-11 NKJV). My hand is literally shaking over the keys of my laptop thinking about the condition of the world had Jesus thought low and gave in to the temptations of the tempter. Life as we know it would not exist.

It is critical not to ignore a very important lesson that is inter-nested in this story. The scripture says that Jesus had been fasting and was hungry when the tempter came. It is fascinating to me that when challenges of the human experience show-up (e.g., finances, illness, conflict with others, etc.) we resist "thinking up" and instead fall to the fray of the challenge or our lower selves. When we face challenges, low thinking can produce temptations that appear as solutions, opportunities, and even a chance of a lifetime. It becomes even more important in these situations to "up" your thinking and remember the promise: the Christ will never lead you to or leave you in temptation.

When you "up" your thinking, you attract like "up thinkers" to you. Up thinkers are jovial and gregarious. Up thinkers are positive and see the glass full whether there is water in it or not. Up thinkers make you laugh and go out of their way to be helpful and supportive. They are encouraging and focus on the possible instead of the impossible. Most importantly, up thinkers are peace makers. They cannot help themselves. And this peace is uncommon and spiritual. It's the kind of peace that Paul refers to being hard to conceive. "And the peace of God which passeth all understanding...," (Philippians 4:7 ESV). Up thinkers bring a peace that makes others feel calm. All hell can be breaking loose around them, but they let nothing disturb them. People look at up thinkers and scratch their heads, questioning what matter of man is this? Why do I feel so calm and peaceful when you're around?

The opposite of up thinking is down thinking. These are the people we'd rather not deal with, at least for long periods of time. The glass is always empty whether there is water in it or not. We say to the down thinker "you are bringing me down" when their conversation is negative and sorrowful. Think about the last time you were invited to a party or social outing. After asking the date, time, and location, what's the next question you ask? Who's going to be there? If it's a bunch or even one down-thinker, you probably choose not to attend.

Just as up thinkers attract other up thinkers, down thinkers love to be around other down thinkers. Up thinkers make down thinkers incredibly uncomfortable. There is genuine pleasure to complain and opine among down thinkers. What would Jesus do? What did Jesus do? Jesus "up-ed" his thinking. What I know for sure is that surrounding myself with up thinkers helps to preserve and express this followership imperative by facilitating peace, harmony and happiness in my relationships.

Love Others

> "Love is patient, love is kind. It does not envy, it does not boast, it is not proud. It is not rude, it is not self-seeking. It is not easily angered, it keeps no record of wrongs. Love does not delight in evil but rejoices in the truth," (1 Corinthians 13:4-6 NIV).

God is love. All the love that is expressed in the universe is therefore pressed out of God. When we express love, we are expressing God. We seek his face or seek his presence when we express love and kindness to others. There are 329,053,135 people in the United States and over seven billion in the world. People show-up in our experience the way they are. They come with their values, beliefs, and opinions. They may come to us as preachers, politicians, or postal workers. Likewise, they come to us as racists, robbers and rioters. However they come, the edict is to love. John implores us to love through a logical argument. He says, "if someone says, I love God but hates a fellow believer, that person is a liar; for if we don't love people we can see, how can we love God, whom we cannot see? And He has given us this command: Those who love God must also love their fellow believers," (1 John 4:20-21 NIV). In other words, if you are walking around proudly boasting of your salvation, presenting yourself as born again, delivered, and redeemed and hate a co-worker, family member, church member, spouse, even the server at your favorite restaurant, you are perpetrating a fraud. You are a liar. For the human being, love is a choice. For the spiritual being (believer) love is an imperative.

This is my first book but certainly not my first experience with people. Because people come as they are with all their stuff, it is challenging to love everybody. I think about old bosses and co-workers who (as I had convinced myself) had one and only one mission in life and that was to make my life a living hell. To love them and show them kindness felt phony and disingenuous. Nonetheless, they were afforded love just like everyone else.

I commute via train to work every day with a routine stop at Starbucks for my triple venti, non-fat, three Splenda extra hot light foam latte. (I love shoes, briefcases and coffee – what can I say). It is sad the way people treat one another. We are rude and disrespectful to each other so much so that when we're not, the loving person is seen as the exception and not the rule. I have witnessed profanity-filled arguments over empty train seats, walking to slowly, mistakes over coffee orders, the blowing of cigarette smoke, and requests for spare change. I've witnessed drivers yelling at each other from one car to another. Train attendants being short with riders. Even pedestrians cursing out Secret Service officers because of an inconvenient presidential or governmental official motorcade delaying their commute to work. There is much love work needed in our society.

Even more disturbing is a lack of love expressed in the church. As I mentioned earlier, I've been a member of someone's church my entire life. I have witnessed a great deal of love in the communities of believers of which I was a member. But conversely, I've seen a lot of hate as well. It is disturbing to me when I see expressions of hate among so-called believers. You cannot pose as saved and holy and all that when you snap at an usher when there are no more printed programs of bulletins, or at a musician for playing a song in the wrong key, or a kitchen worker who gives you white meat chicken when you asked for dark. We should know better and do better. We have a higher standard to conform to. Actions and behaviors that don't express love are out of order.

I courageously submit that it is permissible not to like someone but love them. I am sure the Wayshower did not like everyone He encountered during his earthly assignment, but He was not absent, nor did He ration his love. I do not like some ideas and political posturing of our current president, but I am careful not to say I hate him because that puts me out of order with this principle and the edict of love from the Christ.

When I was a member of the spiritual church, there was a reading we took each Sunday called *Spiritual Communion Service*. I never knew who the author was. I was told that it was a product from the Unity School of Christianity. It was written to emphasize the relevance and importance of the conversations Jesus had with his chosen disciples at the Last Supper rather than the physical (bread and wine). Whoever developed this material was a spiritually-led individual because embedded in the reading is the secret to loving everyone in the world. It reads in part: "The Christ in me beholds the Christ in you. The forgiving love of Jesus Christ fills my mind and heart, and I am at peace with God and man" (Unity, Unknown). The key to loving everyone and expressing God is to find the Christ in them. Allow your Christ spirit to connect with their Christ spirit and express to them love and kindness. The Christ lives in us all. Some express the Christ differently, nonetheless, no human being is absent of the Christ. If we cannot connect with someone on politics, race relations, or even interpretations of scripture, we can always look past what we're seeing through our senses and connect with the Christ within them. In doing so, we forgive them and ourselves for our thinking about them. Doing so helps us realign ourselves with the edict of Jesus – love ye one another.

In one of my work experiences, I encountered an older employee – we'll call her Nancy. She had been with the organization for nearly 25 years and promoted herself as the "go to person" for any and everything. Nancy was feared more than revered and respected. As such, she had a lot of influence among the staff and the ears of upper management. When I started, people warned me not to cross her. People who crossed Nancy, I was told, were soon unemployed.

One day I received a call from her. Her boss wanted a print out of all the employees in the office and their current salaries whether they were in his span of control or not. It was close to merit increase time, and he wanted to make sure his people were being compensated fairly as compared to others. I informed Nancy that I would give her boss the information for people in his area only, as the salary information for others was confidential and proprietary. I emphasized the words to him as she was not privy to that information either. She told me that she had been working in this organization before I was born and was outraged and insulted at the mere hint of her inability to handle confidential information. I explained my intent and trusted she would use her 25-year tenure as a seasoned professional to understand my response. As you may have already surmised, I was not afraid of Nancy.

Fifteen minutes later, I saw her walk into my boss's office and shut the door. Fifteen minutes after that, she left, and my boss came into my office. She told me that I was correct in not supplying the information as requested but warned that I had just acquired a formidable enemy in Nancy. After that, I would see her in the hall or in the elevator, and she'd ignore me. I'd speak to her, and she would walk right by me and not respond. It was also evident that she had broadcast her dislike towards me to other employees. I'd get comments often about how I had made a tremendous mistake of crossing her and my days were surely numbered. None of this phased me. God put me on that job and only God could move me out.

One day she came into HR to complete some forms and I happened to be the only person in our area to help her. My boss and the HR administrative assistant were both out. I asked her if I could help her, and she said no. She'd wait until someone competent could help her. I had had enough. I told her that I didn't care how many years she had been there or how much power she thought she had, she didn't get to disrespect me, defame my character or call my competence into question. I told her that I was not afraid of her and if she thought I was, she was once again mistaken. Her reaction stunned me. She began to cry, and I began to let my anger subsided. I attended to her. I began to look past all the disrespect and anger and connect with her as one spiritual being to the other. I saw a woman who was afraid. The world was moving at a rapid pace, and she was struggling to keep up. Her computer skills were woefully lacking, and she was frightened for her job. I assured her that I could get her the training she needed and that she would be fine. She was better for a few days but began exhibiting her same old behaviors. Rumor had it that she had moved her antics to another employee. But when I did see her, I'd speak and attend to her. You see, at one point, I had begun hating Nancy but when she cried in my presence, I was able to look past her exterior and hard shell to find the Christ in her. I didn't see her as Nancy the mean trouble-maker. I saw her as a sister in Christ. There is another statement of spiritual communion service that I realized: *"We are spiritual being you and I, dwelling together in the harmony of spirit."* And so it is.

The Repentance Imperative – Turn from Your Wicked Ways

> *"But if a wicked man turns from all his sins which he has committed, keeps all my statutes and does what is lawful and right, he shall surely live and shall not die. None of the transgressions which he has committed shall be remembered against him because of the righteousness which he has done, he shall live,"* (Ezekiel 18:21-23 NKJV).

Exercising and demonstrating wicked ways is a major deterrent to your land being healed or to prosperity, good health, and happiness. Have you ever stopped and thought about your ways? I define "ways" as how you operate and express your beliefs and values even when no one is looking. We can be swift to appraise and label the ways of others, but neither helps you nor them grow. Salvation and good living are personal. It's all about what you think about yourself.

The Merriam-Webster Dictionary defines "wicked" as "causing or likely to cause harm, distress, or trouble." This definition comes with a myriad of synonyms which illustrate the meaning more clearly.

A few examples:

Sinful	Immoral	Wrong
Bad	Iniquitous	Corrupt
Ungodly	Irreligious	Profane
Blasphemous	Mean	Vile
Unpleasant	Foul	Nasty
Irksome	Annoying	Abominable
Diabolical	Messy	Detestable

As I wrote those words, images of certain people flashed in my mind. As you read the list, I'm sure you had a similar experience. So now we're done with those people and their ways. Let's now turn to ourselves. Think about your ways again considering the aforementioned definition and list of synonyms. If any of these words can be used to describe your ways, even in part or inconsistently, there is work for you to do. If this definition or these words in no way describe you, there is still work to do in maintaining your progress to live and demonstrate this imperative. This work is the only way we can reach our "new creature" consciousness. The Apostle Paul wrote, "therefore, if anyone is in Christ, he is a new creature; old things have passed away; behold all things have become new," (2 Corinthians 5:17 KJV).

But I didn't write this book to tear myself or anyone down. I come with some good news, news to give you hope and help and build you up. Right now in this very moment, you can make a decision to turn from your wicked ways. This is the essence of repentance (changing your mind and actions to align with Godly values and ideas). Repentance is not complicated or overly involved. You don't have to sit on a special bench in the church, or attend a certain number of special classes, nor wear a particular garment. If any of your ways are wicked, it simply requires you to change your mind and then turn away from them. And because the Father is so merciful, so forgiving, and so gracious, he will help you turn away. His power and might give you strength on your journey to becoming a new creature.

Repentance is an imperative because it realigns us with what God wants us to be – like Him. Because God is good, we are destined for success when our ways reflect His goodness. I am a new creature and thinking new thoughts about God, but I have not deceived myself. We cannot continue to fool ourselves to think that we authentically express Christ and our wicked ways at the same time. James said, "a double-minded man is unstable in all his ways," (James 1:18 KJV). Furthermore, we cannot expect to reap a harvest of blessings with dirt (wickedness) on our hands and hearts. "For the Lord God is a sun and shield; the Lord will give grace and glory; no good thing will He withhold from those who walk uprightly," (Psalms 84:11 KJV).

When you make the decision to repent, you must be crystal clear on what is required. You must understand and accept that your wicked ways are not intended to harm you. They are exercised and directed at other people. We are not foul, iniquitous, and nasty toward ourselves. Our wicked ways are directed to someone or something. Just as others are impacted by your ways, others are involved in your repentance. I submit that true and authentic repentance follows forgiveness, renouncing vengeance, and uses the law of sowing and reaping.

Forgiveness

> *"For if you forgive men their trespasses, your heavenly Father will also forgive you. But if you do not forgive men their trespasses, neither will your Father forgive your trespasses," (Matthew 6:14-15 KJV).*

For reasons of ease, we have convinced ourselves that our wicked ways are justified toward others because they have harmed us or done us wrong. We trick ourselves into believing that it's okay to be vile, combative, and nasty to someone who has exhibited vile, combative, and nasty behaviors toward us. We've altered the golden rule to mean do unto others as they do unto us. Crucify that thought. Cross it out and cancel it now. Whether you are the giver or receiver of wickedness, forgiveness is all about you. You are held to the standard and requirement for how you treat others not how you are treated by others. Remember what Reverend Cobbs advised every Sunday night on his broadcast, "it makes no difference what you think of me, but it does make a difference what I think of you." It makes a difference what I think of you because I must do so to the standard and requirement of the God in me.

There is a woman in my life who always insults me about my weight. I cannot be in her presence for more than 15 minutes without her telling me how big and fat I am. It is mean for her to do so. And although I have lost a great deal of weight, she cannot erase the old images of my morbid obesity from her mind. Her words are so sharp and hurtful, it's difficult to even write about them. In what I used to claim as defense, I used to be ugly, negative and insulting right back to her. I had to learn how to change my thoughts and reactions to her words. In my thoughts and in my words, responses usually ended with "…and you ain't so skinny your damn self." I had to crucify that approach. I had to cross it out. I had to learn not to treat her as she treated me but treat her the way that God wants me to treat her and everyone else in my experience: with love and kindness. That's the master teacher's requirement.

The healing of our land requires us to turn from our wicked ways by forgiving our testers and ourselves. When we hold on to hurt, pain, resentment, anger, hate, etc., it harms us more than it harms the offender. How you are treated is not a part of the equation relative to your salvation and the healing of your land. We want God to be pleased with our actions and reactions and less concerned about the actions and reactions of others. In my example, I forgave her just as she was. As I learned through my spiritual education to affirm, it is not what you think but what I think that makes it so. I've even started saying it to her. I forgive her from saying those hurtful things to me and I forgive myself for every vile and negative response and thought.

Repentance without forgiveness is empty. It means nothing. Forgiveness is at the core of turning from ungodly thinking and actions and aligning yourself with thinking and actions indicative of your understanding of the Christ within you. There is an old adage that confession is good for the soul. That may be true but I'm a believer that forgiveness is even better. Consider what true forgiveness does. Forgiveness:

- Stops us from reliving the seemingly wrong that has been done to us and frees us to live fully in the present;
- Helps us to please God over man/woman, thus setting us up for more good to come our way;
- Let's us regain our personal power. Our anger, regret, hatred, or resentment towards someone means that we are giving-up our power to that person. I have found that while I'm crying, wringing my hands, and pacing the floor about the situation, I'm the farthest thing from offender's mind;
- Brings us back to good physical and mental health. Anger, regret, hate and wickedness on many levels can show up in our bodies. Forgiveness eradicates even the threat of sickness and disease from our bodies and minds.
- Makes it easier to see the God in others. We pray for others and for ourselves with the forgiving love of the Christ within us. As Jesus said on Calvary, "…Father forgive them for they do not know what they are doing," (Luke 23:34 KJV).

You may ask how do I know when I have truly forgiven my offender? People say we should forgive and forget but I disagree. I think we should forgive and remember. We should remember so we can compare how hard it used to be to forgive and now with awareness, understanding and practice, we find ease in forgiving and demonstrating this imperative. There is an old song of the church, entitled *How I Got Over*: My soul looks back and wonder how I got over. The intent of the song reflects on the transition from earth to heaven. When I sing those words, I reflect on how I've learned and spiritually matured. I'm over those old thoughts and beliefs. I'm over feeling inferior. I'm over holding on to those wicked ways of my past. My soul looks back and I <u>know</u> how I got over – with the Christ in me.

Renounce Vengeance

"Do not repay anyone evil for evil. Be careful to do what is right in the eyes of everyone. If it is possible, as far as it depends on you, live at peace with everyone," (Romans 12:17-18 NIV).

Of all the things I needed to work on relative to my spiritual transformation, renouncing vengeance was absolutely the most difficult to master. You are reading the words of a reformed vengeful individual. If someone did or said something to intentionally hurt me, I was determined to get even, get them back, get my revenge. I even had the audacity to pray and ask God to get them for me. My thinking (at the time) was if you mistreat me, surely you could and would handle being mistreated. In my defense, I felt it was my right and my responsibility to make sure they paid for what they did or said to me. And when I heard about something misfortunate happening to them, I immediately attributed their misfortune to my vengeful thoughts showing up and demonstrating as confusion and mayhem in their life.

I know now that this tit-for-tat spirit of vengeance did not serve me well. It created (what I call) a cycle of wickedness. Someone does something to me, I get them back, they in turn get me back and the cycle continues. This is wrong error-filled thinking and not pleasing to God. It's also extremely dangerous and can result in injury, sickness or even death. This is how so-called gangsters and those with criminal minds work, often at the peril of innocent people. Now I am not naïve nor delusional. To turn the other cheek or walk away from your tester or enemy is extremely difficult. But no matter how satisfied and vindicated we feel, we are not at peace with our spiritual selves nor the God-principles that we've been given to follow.

So how do we renounce vengeance? We do so by focusing on the big picture which is what pleases God. Renouncing vengeance is predicated on our understanding of the difference between carnal assurance and blessed assurance. Consider this wisdom from the great prophet Isaiah. "No weapon formed against you shall prosper, and every tongue which rises against you in judgment you, shall condemn. This is the heritage of the servants of the Lord and their righteousness is for me says the Lord," (Isaiah 54:17 KJV).

At the very core of every vengeful act lies the need for assurance that the object of our revenge will pay and atone for their words and acts towards us. We look for signs and evidence of their challenge and suffering and attribute it to the vengeful thoughts and actions we've sent their way. This is carnal assurance. In it, there is erroneous but instant gratification and assurance that they are paying for what they've done. With blessed assurance, we don't rely on our senses or our carnal thinking relative to our tester. We rely on principle, that which is absolute truth and cannot be disproved. Isaiah affirms that if you come against me (an unashamed believer and follower of Godly principles), you will not succeed. It may feel like you're getting away with something but you're not. You will at some point need to atone for your wicked ways and actions towards me.

In this blessed assurance, we don't look for signs and evidence of the other person's suffering or challenge. We don't need to. We affirm (stand firm on) this principle and go free.

This is what David meant when he said, "…make thine enemies they footstool," (Psalms 110:1 KJV). Your enemies don't become your footstool through physical violence. A footstool is used to raise you up. When we deal with our enemies and testers using Godly principles, we step on the experience and get closer to God (higher awareness). And when we are aligned, connected, and attuned to God, we are destined for prosperous and abundant living in freedom and peace.

Understand the Power of Sowing and Reaping

> "Be not deceived. God is not mocked, for whatsoever a man soweth, that shall he also reap," (Galatians 6:7 KJV). "Don't be misled – you cannot mock the justice of God. You will always harvest what you plant," (Galatians 6:7 NLV).

We established earlier in the book that the only power, the only presence in the universe is God the omnipotent – the everywhere present intelligent spirit of absolute good. Through His grace, He gives us so much good that it's impossible to think that we've somehow earned this well-spring of goodness. The old idea of a mean and wrathful old man sitting in the sky prescribing death and suffering for sins is gone. We crucify those old thoughts. We cross them out. We know instead that God gives us purpose and abundance. Paul reminds us, however, that this amazing grace does not dismiss choice and consequence of choice. In this principle of sowing and reaping, all our decisions bring with them a set of results. We cannot lie to ourselves (or be deceived) and think that because of this grace, we are free to do as we please (sin) and all will be okay. That would be mocking God. For the believer and non-believer the universal law is always active irrespective of who you are and what your religious views and practices are.

Some people refer to Karma when describing the principle of sowing and reaping. According to the Lexico-Oxford Dictionary, "Karma" is defined as "in Hinduism and Buddhism the sum of a person's actions in previous states of existence, viewed as deciding their fate in future existences." Not to be flippant nor disrespectful to my Hindu or Buddhist brothers and sisters but Karma is not in my bible; however, the principle of sowing and reaping is. What you send out into the universe comes back greater than how it was sent.

The concept is easily understood through Paul's reference to farming. In the Spring, a farmer plants greens, tomatoes, corn and other vegetables. After several months in the soil and with proper nurturing, his efforts yield acres of food, which is picked, sold, bought, and prepared. Reaping is not a surprise to the farmer. He expects to harvest exactly what he planted but in larger yields. If he plants corn, in four to six months, he expects to harvest corn. And he doesn't expect small scrawny stalks with two or three cobs. He expects tall, healthy, strong stalks weighted down by big, juicy, and vibrant cobs of corn. Likewise, with watermelon, beans, greens – he expects high yields of whatever he plants.

So it is with our thoughts and actions towards our brother and sisters. When we sow patience, love, kindness, acceptance and all the other God-like attributes (seeds) we will receive those things returned pressed down, shaken together, and running over. When you sow your time, energy, money, and knowledge to help someone get through a challenge or crisis, or even offer a kind word or smile to someone who is down and in need of uplifting, it (good) comes back to you in whatever form in which you need it most. And it comes back bigger, louder, greater, and better than what you planted and at the time you need it.

When I lived in Oak Park, Illinois, a suburb of Chicago, I commuted by train into the city each day for work. Each day I would pass a woman sitting on a stool in front of the opera house. I usually don't pay much attention to "pan handlers" but for some reason, this woman caught my attention. Maybe it was her sign which read, "please take my resume. I really need a job." Most people passed her by, but a few people dropped change and a few bills in her collection container. I learned from reading her resume that her name was Mary. One day I stopped and chatted with Mary because I wanted to know her story. How could someone end up in the situation she was in? She informed me that she was a legal secretary for many years until she became ill and could no longer work. She lost her job and then it was downhill from there. She wasn't able to pay her rent and was eventually evicted from her apartment. She said she took to the streets because she didn't know what else to do. I was sad for Mary but in awe of her at the same time. She was always so positive and cheerful, smiling and thanking those who gave her money and took her resume. She would often say to people, "I'd rather have a job than that change but thank you for the change." I felt compelled to help her so every Friday on my way home from work, I'd give Mary a crisp $10.00 bill thinking that she could at least have one decent meal during the week. I couldn't help but think about the old House Music song by the group Machine, *There but For the Grace of God Go I.* When I wasn't rushing to be on time for work in the mornings, I'd stop and talk with Mary and in the cold Chicago winter months, I'd bring her coffee from time to time. She was always "up" and gregarious, which considering her circumstances was amazing. One Friday on my way to work I noticed that Mary wasn't in her normal position in front of the opera house. That evening on the way home I went past her normal post, and she was not there. I prayed that the same mercy and grace that kept her all these months would continue to keep her. I rejoiced for her. Maybe she had found a job and was able to lift herself out of homelessness. I felt in my spirit that she was okay.

In July of that same year, 2015, I accepted a vice president position with my current employer in Washington, D.C. In doing so, I had the awesome task of relocating myself and my family to D.C. In a short amount of time, I had to find temporary housing as I left first, long-term housing for the family when they'd come, tenants for our home in Oak Park, and a job for my wife in D.C. In other words, it was reaping time. It was time to harvest some good I had sown and that's exactly what I did. In a six-week period, we had renters for our Oak Park home, temporary housing for me in D.C., a 5000 square foot home for the family in a D.C. suburb, a job for my wife, a car for my youngest daughter, and new furniture for the home that was twice the size of our home in Oak Park. I felt like I had the golden touch. Everything just worked out and good, good and more good poured in through the doors and windows of my experience. Somewhere along the way (I like to think it was through my Mary experience) I sowed some good into the lives of others and now it was coming back to me bigger, louder, and greater than I could have imagined. The value of my harvest was certainly more than the four or five hundred dollars I had given Mary throughout the year. In fact, I can't even place a value on my harvest. The principle and truth of God's promise worked to bring me the good I needed and even more.

Imagine a world where people (all people) chose to sow good. There would be so much good expressed (sown) and so much received (reaped) that it would simply be incredible. There would be no crime or violence. There would not be room for hatred and prejudice. Again, it would be an incredible experience. But unfortunately, that is not plausible. Because of free will and choice, there are people who choose to sow bad: malice, disruption, hate and a myriad of awful non-good seeds toward others. It's sad to accept that there are some people who thrive on issues and conditions that are vile, mean, and negative. Envy and jealousy cause people to sow bad seeds because of a lack of spiritual understanding. I say again, we live in a universe of lavish abundance. There is enough abundance to go around. There is no need to be envious or jealous of your neighbor or friend because they have attained something that you want.

It is possible for you to have the desires of your heart without negative impact or consequences for your neighbor. There is plenty.

We often sow bad when we think that someone is being blessed or moving ahead, and we think they shouldn't or that they don't deserve it. How did he or she get a better score on that exam than I did? How are they able to afford that luxury car when I earn more than they earn? How was he or she able to meet and marry their spouse and I wasn't? The pondering and declaration of why them and not me stems from a spirit of competition that people unnecessarily create in their minds. These unhealthy thoughts and ways of thinking breed bad seeds. And these seeds go out as thoughts and actions to attack others.

It is extremely dangerous to work with this sowing and reaping principle in a negative downward manner because what is sown has to grow and be harvested. Those thoughts and acts of malice, jealousy, and the like that we send out show-up in our experiences, bigger and more profound than we send them. And unlike the positive affirmative harvest from sowing good, we are never ready for the harvest of bad. There is never the right or perfect time to reap discord in our lives. But God is not mocked – you get back what you send out, pressed down, shaken together, and running over.

Now that you've come into this awareness, I challenge you to cancel negative thoughts and deceitful plans and plots against others. No matter what they've done or said to you, cancel those thoughts and plots and instead sow good. It may appear difficult in some cases not to be vengeful and unforgiving but like anything else important to your highest good, it's worth it. Sewing negative and bad intended seeds reap more to the sower than the other person. Not only will you reap what you sow, you will become what I refer to as "spiritually disturbed." Spiritual disturbance occurs when you let any down-thinking thought or challenge pull you away from Godly ideals, truths and principles. This pulling often manifests itself as heated arguments, physical abuse, gossip, subterfuge, all of which requires energy away from thinking and doing the right thing. In this spiritually disturbed state, we compromise our peace. And not the peace that's satisfied with material things but a peace that comes from freedom, God, and what Paul describes as a peace "...which passeth all understanding and keeps our hearts and minds through Christ Jesus," (Philippians 4:7 KJV). When these thoughts and occurrences show-up, I quickly work to cancel them with an affirmation. I remember hearing these words from the late Rev. Dr. Johnnie Colemon. "I will let nothing, no -thing, or person disturb the calm peace of my soul." In other words, I refuse to allow your inconsequential attacks, hate-motivated words and actions pull me way from my personal and spiritual good of living a happy, healthy and prosperous life. My eyes and entire consciousness in focused on sewing good and not on unforgiving, vengeful and hateful thoughts about you and your opinions of me. Your seeming threats against my peace are rebuked. I go away from you and your "messiness" just as I came: free and unharmed.

Becoming a practitioner of these imperatives (i.e., humility, prayer, seeking his face, and turning from your wicked ways) may require you to turn away from some people. When I embraced these new thoughts, several people who were important in my life couldn't handle me thinking differently from them. I was characterized as being brain-washed, a member of a cult, a victim of the devil and even a heretic. If or when this happens, you will have to make some important decisions about your relationships, many of which you have cultivated over decades. You will have to choose between compromising what you know now as truth and conforming to traditional and widely acceptable religious beliefs. I encourage you to choose truth over conformity. A choice of truth is a choice for your soul. As Mark asserts, "For what shall it profit a man if he shall gain the whole world and lose his own soul?" (Mark 8:36 KJV).

The law of purpose suggests that things and people come into our experience with a purpose. Acceptance to a college or university comes with a purpose of providing learning and mastery of a certain body of knowledge to prepare us for a career. A man or woman may come to marriage with the purpose of having companionship, love, and even children. On a more mundane level, a television comes for entertainment and in some cases information and education. In taking people and things into our lives, it is important to spend some time clearly discerning its purpose. This discerning is important because once a thing or person fulfills that purpose, it will separate from us. It does this to make room for the next purposeful person or thing.

In a previous job, things went from being smooth and easy to rough and hard. At the same time, recruiters were calling me about new opportunities. One of the opportunities came with 800 employees and a large HR staff to manage. I had never managed a team that large nor supported a workforce of that magnitude. I took that position and after 18 months, I left that position for another. I know now that the first job gave me individual contributor experience and the latter gave me large-staff experience, both which have contributed to my success in my current job. God will lead you to people, places and things to prepare you for future success. You'll ask yourself why in the world did God bring this person into my life? What was I thinking? Why did I take this job? That person and that job came to prepare you for something bigger and better. That's how He works. There is no need to be angry or frustrated when things and people have fulfilled their purpose and separate from us. The omniscience of God is at work, and we move at his guidance and direction. I believe this is what Paul meant when he advised that "...all things work together for good to those who love God, to those who are called according to His purpose," (Romans 8:28 NKJV).

In conclusion as I reflect on this chapter, I feel a certain level of expertise and wisdom relative to these imperatives, not as an author but as a practitioner. I've walked through and lived through these lessons. I've lived through trying to serve and help others and be discouraged and alienated for doing so. I know how difficult it is to let God handle it instead of seeking vindication and revenge. I have experienced the up-thinking in consciousness from inferiority (thinking less of myself) to humility (thinking of myself less). It's a journey with multiple opportunities to learn. But what I've discovered is that challenges bring the lessons and the lessons bring growth and development. And God the good has provided illumination and increase every step of the way. I encourage you to work with these imperatives and set out anew on your journey so you can rise to this pinnacle level of understanding and strong alignment with God.

Think on These Things

1. Describe how acknowledgement as outlined in this chapter is a demonstration of humility?
2. Explain why worrying is counter-productive to praying.
3. How would you describe the dynamic of "up-thinking" to your friend or colleague?
4. Relative to sowing and reaping, what does it mean to mock God?
5. What does "followership" mean and why should it be an imperative to better living?
6. Vengeance can initiate a "cycle of wickedness." Explain.

CHAPTER 7

I Shall Not Want

• • ● • •

> "The Lord is my Shepard. I shall not want," (Psalms
> 23:1 KJV)
> "The Lord is my Shepard. I lack nothing," (Psalms 23:1
> NIV)
> "The Lord is my Shepard. I will always have everything
> I need," (Psalms 23:1, Easy-to-Read Version – ERV)

David not only affirms his conviction here, but he summarizes the underlying and underpinning purpose, power and presence of this book: If I believe, accept, and practice God the good omnipotent, omnipresent, and omniscient as my Shepard (guide, protector, and provider) I will never want for a thing. If I allow God to be my Shepard, every good and perfect thing I desire is already mine. My life, through God, will be full of happiness, good health and wealth. The transformation that we all strive for is possible when we view God differently – from the vantage point of a renewed mind.

In my still and quiet, I began meditating on how I wanted to conclude this book. What thought or lesson or feeling did I want to leave with all those who read it? My mind immediately filled with all sorts of ideas, which was frankly overwhelming. I stepped away knowing that Spirit would bring me the answer because that's what Spirit does. Several days later, I saw my father's face and heard his voice in consciousness. This happened a few times during the day. I said aloud, what does this mean?

And as clear and plain as if another person was speaking to me in person, I heard his voice saying, "write about prosperity." I couldn't help but chuckle. Not to defame him or his reputation but Larry Robertson Sr. was certainly not the poster child for prosperity. He struggled financially until the day of his demise. Also clear and just as plain, I heard him say, "maybe a lesson from you will prevent people from living as I lived – in lack and in sickness." I thought about it: this entire rendering is about what I've learned and know for sure about God. It would be incomplete without my thoughts on prosperity.

There are so many definitions, models, and plans on the subject of prosperity, it's no wonder that the novice or those seeking basic but comprehensive knowledge are easily and quickly confused. Equally plentiful are misconceptions, assumptions, and so-called ministries about prosperity. In reality, it's really not that hard of a concept to understand. As you have learned from reading this book, I believe in making things as clear and easy to understand as possible. I define prosperity as the sustaining favor and ever-flowing output of absolute good from the God source to me. Prosperity is the constant and continual flow of God's goodness to me however I need it. I describe the flow as continual because there is no concern or fear of shortage. There is enough good for every human being on the face of the earth to enjoy and even more to spare. God is the source and not the channel. Channels bring my good to me and although channels can dry up or even disappear, new channels are created for the sole purpose of bringing good to me. In the last chapter, Calvin was a channel by which the home financing came. God was the source.

Although prosperity includes money, it's bigger than money. Money is important. It is a common form of payment for goods and services all over the world. When Solomon wrote in Ecclesiastes that, "a feast is made for laughter, and wine makes life merry, but money is the answer for everything," (Ecclesiastes 10:19 NIV), he was operating in one realm of consciousness, the carnal. In our carnal minds, we see money as the answer to all the problems we could ever have but this is error thinking. As the constant and continual flow of God's goodness to me, prosperity is whatever I need, want, or desire to my highest good. Wealth is prosperity, but wealth cannot heal my body. Good health is prosperity, but it can't pay my bills. There is really no such thing as one-dimensional prosperity. This flow of good comes as an answer to our prayers in the right form. It's the favor of God. It's the fulfillment of a promise. It's the reward for our success and even for our efforts to live by Godly principles and practices.

Some of you won't like this but when I think of prosperity, I can't help but to think of the prophetic ministry of the late Reverend Frederick Eikerenkotter better known as Reverend Ike. Back in the 60s and 70s when prosperity teaching was dismissed and even frowned upon by popular religious and denomination leaders, Reverend Ike was evangelizing about the possibility of God's children living full and complete lives and having happiness, good health, success and all the money they could handle. His motto was, "you can't lose with the stuff I use." Many people dismissed him, laughed at him and even mocked him. They didn't care much about this "stuff" he used. When fundamentalists realized that the "stuff" he used was biblical and reflected the true will of God for His children, this prosperity doctrine was widely accepted. Now in 2019, ten years after his transition, ministers in most denominations are preaching health, wealth, and success. In one of his many interviews, he unapologetically clarified his approach and goal.

> "I'm not trying to gather followers unto myself. It has never been my purpose to herd the masses into the folds of organized religion. My purpose is to bring the individual to an awareness of his own in-dwelling divinity and to believe in the God within. I'm trying to get people of all races and religions to believe in themselves so correctly and so positively that they can be independent spiritually, mentally, and economically," (Your Key, 2019).

In essence, Reverend Ike wanted for us exactly what we want for ourselves: to live a life as a child of God in happiness and abundance. I refer to his ministry as prophetic because he was able to see years ago where we are now; building a consciousness of abundance.

The good news I bring is that prosperity is possible (able to happen), plausible (reasonable to happen) and probable (more likely than unlikely to happen) for the believer. I will even go as far as to say that it is impossible to be a true follower of Christ and not be prosperous. As a convicted believer, we are, as Joshua said, prosperous and successful by living according to the imperatives and principles of God. I know for certain that prosperity is God's will for all that believe, therefore His will for me. "Beloved, I pray that you may prosper in all things and be in good health, just as your soul prospers," (3 John 1:2 NKJV).

It is sad to think that some people reject the idea of the sustaining favor and ever-flowing output of absolute good from the God source. There are people who would rather believe in lack and long-suffering as a means to validate their conviction and salvation. I can unequivocally and without trepidation claim that this is incorrect thinking. This thinking needs to be crucified right out of your thinking. We are a chosen and peculiar people: we believe in a God we cannot see. It was not the disciples, nor the great prophet Isaiah, nor the emancipator Moses, nor any other prominent biblical leader but it was the Lord who said, I did not come to slay you, nor condemn you, nor shame you, nor take away from you. "The thief's purpose is to steal and kill and destroy. My purpose is to give them a rich and satisfying life," (John 10:10 NLT).

This continual flow from God comes to whomever is ready and able to receive it. You don't have to be a certain race, color, age or religion to receive it. There is no special certification or degree required. You don't need a candle, incense or the lottery numbers to get it. All that is required is an awareness of happiness, health, and wealth and a drive to live a life that pleases God. "So do not worry saying what shall we eat or what shall we drink or what shall we wear. For the pagans run after all these things, and your heavenly Father knows that you need them. But seek first His kingdom and His righteousness, and all these things will be given to you as well," (Matthew 6:31-33 NIV). I'm excited about these things. I want these things in my body warding of all disease and ailments. I want these things in my relationships and business affairs to realize growth and success. I want these things in my wallet and bank accounts to draw to me all the money my consciousness can accept. Health, wealth, happiness and money to my highest good are pressed out of God the good. That's just the way it is.

As I prepared to write this chapter and pull together all my research, I asked myself a simple but important question: what do I know for sure about prosperity? What can I impart to my readers about this God-promised gift and state of being? This is what I know for sure.

God Wants Us to Prosper

> *"For I know the plans I have for you, declares the Lord, plans to prosper you and not harm you, plans to give you hope and a future," (Jeremiah 29:11 NIV).*

It is empowering, energizing, and reassuring to know that God's plan for me is health, wealth and happiness however I need or want it. He is good by nature and has plans for me to receive as much good as I desire. His will for me is absolute good. So now I will reject the old ideas and teachings of a God who inflicts sickness, sorrow and suffering. Those things are the opposite of His nature. His plan for me is to prosper. There is a place inside of you where everything is well, whole, and perfect. Go to that place and draw into your experience all the prosperity that God has planned for you. Affirm: God's plan for me is absolute and abundant good.

Our Father Is the King

> *"And he answering said to his father, lo, these many years do I serve thee, neither transgressed I at any time thy commandment and yet thou never gavest me a kid, that I might make merry with my friends. But as soon as thy son was come, which hath devoured thee living with harlots, thou have killed for him the fatted calf. And he said unto him, son thou art ever with me and <u>all that I have is thine.</u> It was meant that we should make merry and be glad; for this thy*

brother was dead and is alive again, and was lost and is found," (Luke 15:29-32 KJV).

Jeff Bezos, founder of Amazon, is said to be the richest person in the world with an estimated net worth of $131 billion dollars. Bill Gates, founder of Microsoft, ranks as the second richest with an estimated net worth of $96.5 billion dollars. Warren Buffet, owner of GEICO Insurance, Duracell, Dairy Queen and more than 60 other companies makes the list with an estimated net worth of $82.5 billion. Mark Zuckerberg, founder of Facebook has wealth estimated at $62.3 billion. The richest woman, Francoise Bettencourt Meyers, granddaughter to the L'Oréal Cosmetics founder, Eugene Schueller, has an estimated net worth of $49.3 billion. How ridiculous would it be to think that the children and grandchildren of the world's wealthiest people would ever be in financial need. Why? Because their fathers and grandfathers, mothers and grandmothers are rich. All that they need (materially) is possible because their father is rich. What the Bezos, Gates, Buffet, Zuckerberg, and Meyers families have in wealth is but a morsel or mustard seed portion of what our heavenly Father has. And His plan for us is absolute good and abundance. How ridiculous, then, it is for us, the children of God to ever worry about our financial needs. And above these billionaires, our father is omnipotent, which means He has the power to provide all we need (health, happiness, and wealth).

Our Father is the king. All we could ever want, or need is possible. He is the source of all good and "...it is your Father's good pleasure to give you the kingdom," (Luke 12:32 KJV). We are heirs to all our Father has. Our true lineage is divine. We suffer and accept lack and limitation because we forget our divinity. We forget who our Father is. We are rich and prosperous in every way because our Father is the king and all He has is ours. Affirm: My Father is rich and all He has is mine.

We Live in a World of Immeasurable Good

> "Now to Him who is able to do immeasurably more
> than all we ask or imagine, according to His power that
> is at work within us," (Ephesians 3:20 NIV).

Have you ever dealt with someone who tried to cheat or scam you? Have you ever been robbed or taken advantage of in a business deal or agreement? Have you ever had to see someone or seek legal assistance to recover what someone has taken from you? If you haven't, thank God. If you have, like me, then you can surely agree with me that it's one of the worse situations to encounter and recover from.

It is sad to realize that hundreds if not thousands of people make it their full-time job to steal and scam hard-working people out of money. According to the Federal Trade Commission, over three million identity thefts and frauds were reported in 2018. Of the cases reported, approximately 350,000 of them resulted in money loss of approximately $400 million. Maybe scammers take this route to wealth because it is easy. Maybe these methods are quicker and more exciting and more profitable than more conventional means. Whatever the reason, I believe these unscrupulous acts stem from a misconception that there is a shortage of abundance in the universe and requires the creation and execution of fraudulent and illegal tricks and schemes to take from those who have prosperity. This approach and thinking are based on error-thinking: the way to get ahead means taking from those who have gotten ahead.

The truth is that we live in a world of limitless abundance of which God is the source. Therefore, there is no need for theft, fraud, and scamming. All that we could ever need or want comes from God. His riches and resources are immeasurable. He is not a channel of abundance. He is the source of all good and abundance. It all comes from Him.

I was walking out of the barbershop on a recent Saturday afternoon with another patron when a beautiful espresso brown Mercedes S550 passed by us. I said aloud, "that's my car." The gentleman walking with me said, "no that's his car. Your car is still at the dealership. I'm sure he's not driving the only brown Mercedes in the world." He was correct. That was not my car. My car is waiting for me. I don't have to devise some sinister plan to get that driver's car, as there is no shortage of homes, money, or luxury cars in the universe. I need to build the consciousness for whatever I desire, ask with expectancy, and wait for my good to come. The source of infinite and immeasurable good is pleased to give me the kingdom. Oh how different the world would be if everyone had a renewed mind of God as the true source of all good. As the songwriter wrote, "my Father is rich in houses and land, he holds the wealth of the world in His hands, of riches and diamonds, of silver and gold, His coffers are full, His riches untold."

Affirm: All that I need and want is mine from God, the source of immeasurable good!

I Can See My Good

> "Then the Lord said to me write my answer plainly on tablets, so that a runner can carry the correct message to others. This vision is for a future time. It describes the end, and it will be fulfilled. If it seems slow in coming, wait patiently, for it will surely take place. It will not be delayed," (Habakkuk 2:2-3 NLT).

Earlier in the book, I submitted that your imagination was a God-given power leading you in your quest to live a happy, healthy and prosperous life. I reiterate that concept in this point as well. Your consciousness is a giant movie screen, projecting your thoughts and feelings about what has occurred and what is occurring in your life. To be prosperous, we must also visualize our future state as well.

We sit and think about our past and seeming challenges of our present all the time. In doing so, we project the wrong images on our screens, which commands the universe to "send me more." Thinking about your past and present sorrows and pain only brings more sorrow and pain. Why? Because it is what we are projecting to the universe on the screens of our mind. What you project on the screen of your mind is a prayer and desire all in one. You are saying to the universe "this is important to me. This is what I've imagined for myself. This is what I want. Send this!" God has designed a universal system to respond to your prayers and desires. The images in your mind set into action all the people, processes, and circumstances to bring those things to you. Similar to the principle of sowing and reaping, these images are planted in the soil of universal order. They must grow and must be harvested. Those who picture themselves as lonely, abused, mistreated, unworthy, poor, sick, unhappy, bewitched, bothered and bewildered draw those things and feelings back to themselves and in increased form.

Here's the good news: you can change those images. You can imagine and visualize the desires of your heart on your big mind screen. You can project images of wealth, health, and happiness instead of lack, sickness, and sorrow. And when you do, the universe snaps into action to bring it all to you and in increased form. A young lady I knew (we'll call her Leslie) reflecting on her then abusive relationship with her partner demonstrates this point. She said, "I had to first see a day when I was not beaten by him. Then I had to imagine more days. I eventually had an image of my life without abuse and when that day came, I ran like Angela Basset [who played Tina Turner] in the movie *What's Love Got to Do with It*. When I was rid of him, I reflected back on why I didn't leave sooner. I didn't run sooner because I had accepted the abuse as normal. It wasn't until I built the consciousness for a life free from abuse that my real deliverance came. Deliverance is not a shouting and dancing thing. It's a mind thing." Leslie is now married to a great and loving guy and is happy and safe.

Everything (good and not so good) begins in the mind. It's up to us to control our mind images to attract the good that we want and need. When those images, resultant of down-thinking, project on our screen, we must quickly erase them and replace them with positive up-thinking images. It's not easy. It's not easy to recondition your mind and dismiss decades of negative images stemming from negative conditioning. All those years of being told that you were nothing to God, a wretch undone, a worm of the dust, and a poor pilgrim are sitting in your subconscious phase of mind just waiting to pop-up on your screen and erase the goodness and joy you have envisioned for your life. It's not easy to eradicate this conditioning but it is possible.

To help me, I use a vision board. On a large poster board, I find and post images from the Internet and magazines that reflect my heart desires. I include affirmations and positive words with each picture. I place that board in a private but visible place for my eyes only. Every day, morning and night, I go to that board and pray. I touch the pictures and imagine myself already having those things and feelings. I close my eyes and visualize myself wearing it, riding in it, being there and feeling that way. When doubt comes in, I draw a big X through that image and focus on the image that represents my desire. I update my board as things are demonstrated and become my experience.

More good news: It is never too late to begin. Start with some highly specific goals. Don't think about the past but focus on the future. You have already achieved your goal. Create and hold a mental picture of it as if it were occurring to you at that very moment. Imagine the scene in as much detail as possible. Engage as many of your five senses as you can in your visualization. Which emotions are you feeling at that moment? What do you smell, see, taste, hear or touch? Hold that image firm in your mind as you pray. Create or update your vision board to reflect those images. Replace all the negative. Fill your mind and your screen with the pictures which reflect achievement of the goal you envision for yourself and "... calleth those things which be not as though they were," (Romans 4:17 KJV). Affirm: I see my good. I embrace my good. I know my good is on the way. It's already here. Thank You, God.

I Serve a Big God

> "Then Moses stretched out his hand over the sea; and the Lord caused the sea to go back by a strong east wind all that night; and made the sea into dry land, and the waters were divided. So the children of Israel went into the midst of the sea on dry ground, and the waters were a wall to them on their right hand and on their left. And the Egyptians pursued and went after them into the midst of the sea, all Pharaoh's horses, his chariots and his horsemen. Now it came to pass in the morning watch that the Lord looked down upon the

*army of the Egyptians through the pillar of fire and cloud,
and He troubled the army of the Egyptians. And He took
off their chariot wheels, so they drove them with difficulty;
and the Egyptians said, let us flee from the face of Israel,
for the Lord fights for them against the Egyptians. Then
the Lord said to Moses, 'stretch out your hand over the sea
that the waters may come back upon the Egyptians on their
chariots and on their horsemen.' And Moses stretched out
his hand over the sea; and when the morning appeared, the
sea returned to its full depth while the Egyptians were fleeing
into it. So the Lord overthrew the Egyptians in the midst of
the sea. Then the waters returned and covered the chariots,
the horsemen and all the army of Pharaoh that came into
the sea after them. Not so much as one of them remained,"
(Exodus 14:20-28 NKJV).*

Have you ever had a Red Sea experience? Do you know what it is? A Red Sea experience describes a seeming circumstance or situation where your conscious phase of mind cannot see a way to success or safety. It's a situation that appears impossible to overcome. You can't forge ahead, you can't retreat, you can't go left or right. You are stuck. You stand stuck bracing yourself for the danger to come upon you. This was the experience of the Israelites. They thought they would surely die no matter what they did. It was either stay and be slain by the Egyptians or drown in the Red Sea.

A Red Sea experience is not a fading casual annoyance. A Red Sea experience is a situation or a set of circumstances as mammoth as the sea itself. At present, the Red Sea has a surface area of roughly 169,100 miles, is about 1300 miles long, and its width is 220 miles wide. This is not a headache, or an influenza. This is a seemingly unsolvable problem. These mammoth circumstances can show up in your relationships, on your job, in your body and in your wallet or purse. I think of the hundreds of people who thought they were wealthy and prosperous only to learn they were actual victims of Bernard Madoff, who stole and squandered their life savings leaving them with nothing. I think of the women in my life who, after a routine exam, were diagnosed with breast cancer. I think of the thousands of parents, husbands, and wives whose children or spouses are addicted to street or prescription drugs and have literally destroyed their financial security and health because of that addiction. I think about that day in 2013 when my boss, looking across the table at me during lunch, told me that my job was being eliminated for no fully disclosed reason. She said that if I stayed with the organization, she feared I would not grow. Looking back, I think she was probably right but also in looking back, I know it was not the full truth. I think about working all day and coming home and working all night preparing cover letters and sending resumes simply because she no longer wanted me in her organization. The feelings I experienced of failure and embarrassment, coming to work every day, knowing and everyone else knowing that in a matter of weeks, I would be unemployed. Trying to show confidence and a positive disposition while all along feeling wrought with angst and worry about finding another job to support my family was miserable to say the least. Pushing away thoughts of hate and abhorrence about a boss that I once was very fond of almost took me out. No one is in a good place when you have little hope or confidence that you will prevail. This is a Red Sea experience.

But I bring some good news: We, you and I, serve a big God who "…is able to do exceedingly abundantly above all that we ask or think according to the power that worketh in us," (Ephesians 3:20-21 KJV). It irritates me when people make statements like, "God ain't gonna bless me like that," or "everybody can't be rich," or "this thing I have is incurable." Those statements really support an unconscious belief that God is not big enough or able enough to demonstrate in you favor in your life, right where you need Him. Statements such as these signify doubt in the omnipotence of God that we dance and shout about in church every Sunday.

If you change only one thing about your understanding of God from reading this book, I implore you to cancel the thoughts and feelings that support a limited God. He is able to do whatever we ask and then some. The same God that rolled back 220 miles of water is able to heal you. The same God that made a dry road in the middle of the sea can make you a millionaire overnight. And while you're worried about losing that job, God is commanding the universe to create connections and opportunities to acquire a better job or even start your own business. Since that conversation in 2013 with my then boss, I've had two jobs and now serve as a vice president with a salary that is nearly twice the salary, I earned from that job that I was so worried about losing.

I know for sure that it is error-thinking to discriminate in things we take to God. Because his yoke is easy and his burdens are light, He can handle it all. I've learned (and yes, I'll say the hard way) to trust in the Lord with all my heart (my entire consciousness) and lean not unto my own (carnal) understanding. In all my ways, whether a rain puddle experience or a Red Sea experience, I've learned to acknowledge the omnipotence, omnipresence, and omniscience of God and I know that He will direct my path to wholeness and prosperity. Affirm: There is absolutely nothing, no-thing too hard for God. Whatever God can't do, simply cannot done!

My Lexicon Has Power

> *"As the rain and the snow come down from heaven, and do not return to it without watering the earth and making it bud, and flourish, so that it yields seed for the sower and bread to the eater, so is my word that goes out from my mouth; it will not return to me empty, but it will accomplish what I desire, and achieve the purpose for which I sent it,"* (Isaiah 55:10-11 NIV).

The Lexico-Oxford Dictionary defines "lexicon" as "the vocabulary of a person, language or branch of knowledge." Each one of us has a set of words we use in our daily communications be it verbal or written. I have a couple. My lexicon during the week at work with my colleagues is professional and august. On the weekends with family and friends, my words are extremely non-professional and less ostentatious. No matter the setting, professional or relaxed, our lexicon or our vocabulary plays a very important role in establishing wealth, health, and happiness. As

Isaiah stated, our words have power to accomplish what we please. Your words have power and make a unique and distinct impression upon the universe. When you speak, the universe goes into action to accomplish what you speak. Ever wonder why you have so much sorrow? Perhaps it's because you continually say, "I'm sorry." Ever wonder why you are in a perpetual state of lack? Perhaps it's because you are continually declaring yourself as broke. Ever wonder why you can't hold on to feeling good and good health? It may be caused by your continual affirmation of being sick. As a spiritual being, you must understand, accept, and practice the effective power of the words you use.

The Wayshower said that we could speak to a mountain, commanding it to be moved and it will crumble. Because we are masterfully created, God equipped us with this unique power which no other creature possesses. Metaphysically, a mountain represents a seemingly impossible-to-move barrier between us and our health, happiness, and well-being. But those barriers are not truths. Those barriers don't represent our divinity or spiritual lineage. They are not real but illusions. Jesus is telling us to shut down those barriers because we have the power to do so.

Our lexicon should be such that we bring into our lives all the good that we can handle. This is how the earth was created. This is how we were created. God spoke "let there be" and wondrous things began to happen. The good news here is that you have the power within your lexicon to do the same thing. When we model our thoughts, actions, and words to align with the thoughts, actions and words of the Wayshower, we create whatever experience we want. This is the awareness of the God-power within that must be demonstrated in your journey to prosperous living.

Jesus said, "I tell you the truth, anyone who believes in me will do the same works I have done and even greater works, because I am going to be with my Father," (John 14:12 NLT). Jesus reassured the disciples that their journey and their assignments were not over just because he was leaving, rather, they were just beginning. They would remain wealthy. They would remain in good health. They would remain a part of the brotherhood. Water could still be turned into wine. People could still be healed. The hungry could still be fed. All these works and even greater works than these are possible with the Christ presence within. All things are possible. Nothing is impossible. Because of this truth, our words should reflect our knowledge and belief that because God Is able, we are able, worthy, and entitled to good, good, and more good. And yes, I used the word entitled because as children of God, we are entitled to an inheritance of good. Entitlement means that you are to benefit from something not based on your efforts. The prodigal son received a king's welcome, complete with music, his friends, wine, and the fatted calf, the best calf on the farm. He had blown his money and was sleeping and eating with the pigs. But one day, the bible says, "he came to himself," and went back to his rich father. In a church I used to attend, we had a slogan – "prosperity is my birthright." I believe that completely. Use your words and let them bring to you all you want, need, and desire.

Affirm: My words are full of power and bring to me all that I desire!

Giving Brings the Gifts

> *"Remember this: whoever sows sparingly will also reap sparingly, and whoever sows generously will also reap generously. Each of you should give what you have decided on in your heart to give, not reluctantly or under compulsion, for God loves a cheerful giver,"* (2 Corinthians 9:6-7 NIV).

It took me (as the younger generation would say) "a minute" to really understand the close relationship between giving and receiving. In my limited training and selfishness, I didn't understand how one (giving) had anything to do with the other (receiving). What I witnessed was a focus on "getting." It was all about acquiring as much stuff as I could acquire and holding on to it for dear life. The presiding mindset was that a blessing meant getting something for nothing and getting ahead. Giving meant losing, so I had to hold on to whatever I received.

The truth is you cannot boast of being prosperous and having a prosperity consciousness if you are not a cheerful giver. I further submit that you cannot create and sustain a prosperity consciousness if you have not practiced cheerful giving. Just like the farmer we discussed in the previous chapter, it would make absolutely no sense to expect a harvest of watermelons if corn was planted. You harvest (reap) what you've planted (sown). Likewise, it would be foolish to expect abundance when you've sown sparingly or nothing at all.

Giving is an act of faith; faith in the promise that God made of "... opening the windows of heaven and pouring out such blessings that there will not be room enough to receive," (Malachi 3:10 KJV). Giving brings blessings to the giver as well as the receiver. God returns to the giver pressed down, shaken together and running over. Giving initiates the process of circulation. I've learned not to declare money as "spent." When money is spent, it's gone. It's cast away and you will never see again. I've learned to circulate my money. When I give, even in paying my bills, I do so with an expectancy that it will all return to me in an abundant way. I pay my bills and give cheerfully, happily, and freely. That's what God loves, and I can't help but believe that we set ourselves up for supernatural success and prosperity when we act in a manner which pleases God. The late Dr. Mary Tumpkin, former president of the Universal Foundation for Better Living (UFBL) once said during an offering time in her service, "don't get all frowned-up when it's time to give. When the basket comes to you, smile when you drop it [your offering]." Her message emphasized the importance of demonstrating cheerful giving in building a consciousness for prosperity. Smile, be happy, and rejoice because God is putting your harvest in motion.

A few years ago, a few of my buddies and I attended a special service featuring Pastor Jamal Bryant at a church located in a suburb of Chicago. I was well along on my up-thinking journey and really didn't want to spend my Friday night listening to a "fire and brimstone" fundamentalist sermon but the fellas assured me that I wouldn't be disappointed, and they were correct. This man was an awesome vessel for God. As the older saints would say after a good sermon, "he preached the horns off of the alter."

Service began around 7:30 and it was now 11:00 p.m. and time for the offering. My days of long church services have been long gone for a long time, so I was ready to give for more than one reason. I opened my wallet and quickly passed my emergency hundred-dollar bill and pulled out a five-dollar bill for the offering. Giving my emergency hundred-dollar bill never entered my mind. That was my "rainy day" money. If I held on to that I would always have and never be without. Pastor Bryant began ministering about the importance of giving. He suggested that one of the reasons our blessings are "locked-up" is because we fail to give. Giving releases the blessing. Giving brings the gift. It's important to note that this was a time when I was struggling financially. I had some financial obligations that were difficult to meet. I was meeting them but not getting ahead. I was focused on receiving and certainly not giving. He started with the $500 line, then $400, then $300 and so on. I waited patiently for the "whatever you're going to give line," knowing that there would not be a $5 line. As people were walking up to give, he continued ministering about giving and receiving. He spoke about making choices, referencing purchasing the new iPhone (which was $200 back then) or sowing a seed into an anointed ministry. For the first time, I thought about the emergency rainy-day $100 in my wallet and the $5 in my hand, and then he said it. "You are sitting there waiting on God to bless you and will not trust the promise of God to give just a little of what he's given you. You want to pay that bill you're struggling to pay? You want the offer for that new job? You want that house you pass by every day, then exercise your faith. Give and unlock your good." As an act of faith, I pulled out the hundred-dollar bill, added it to the five-dollar bill and got into the line. It wasn't about Pastor Bryant or this church. It was about me and God. I gave truly believing that I was unlocking the good I needed.

In the weeks that followed, I began paying attention and looking for the blessings to come my way. The major debt that I was so concerned about was eliminated just by me calling and asking – Praise God! And the job offer I was waiting on came with a larger salary and even a $5,000 signing bonus – Praise God! I didn't attribute these blessings to Pastor Bryant nor to the lovely young lady I spoke with who all but eliminated my balance on the debt. And although grateful for my new job, I knew that the CEO of my new employer had little to do with my blessing. It was God giving back to me in true harvest fashion the seed I had planted. I know for sure that giving brings the gifts.

It is critical not to stop the cycle of giving and receiving. It is critical to give when you receive. I think about Bill and Melinda Gates, Warren Buffet, Oprah Winfrey and other billionaires who give millions of dollars to schools, churches and humanitarian organizations. They do this to help and assist but I think they give because they understand the law. Non-giving stops the circulation process. Anything that remains still becomes stagnant and losses life. In order to have energy and momentum and life, there has to be movement. There has to be circulation. We stop our financial blessing by letting our money sit still. Money should always be moving, being invested, earning interest, growing and maturing. Saving for a rainy day is stagnation. Learn how to invest and wisely circulate your wealth. As Rev. Ike once said, "I am striving to get to a point in my life where I no longer work for money but money works for me."

Affirm: God's divine love works through me to bless all that I give and all that I receive. My Father is good. He blesses the giver just as the receiver. My good circulates back to me, pressed down, shaken together and running over. Thank you, God.

I Believe in Miracles

> "When He had finished speaking, He said to Simon, put out into deep water and let down the nets for a catch. Simon answered, Master, we've worked hard all night and haven't caught anything. But because you say so, I will let down the nets. When they had done so, they caught such a large number of fish that their nets began to break. So they signaled their partners in the other boats to come and help them, and they came and filled both boats so full they began to sink," (Luke 5:4-6 NIV).

I have loved and enjoyed this "Jesus miracle" story since I was a little boy in Sunday school. I don't know why I was so excited then, but I know why these stories excite me now. They prove and reinforce my belief in miracles.

The Oxford-Cambridge Dictionary defines "miracle" as "an unusual and mysterious event that is thought to have been cause by God." I define a miracle as God working to demonstrate the seemingly impossible. The "great catch" story is interesting to me because it was a double-miracle. The disciples did not use rods or baited hooks. They simply dropped their nets, hoping that a large school of fish would be trapped, thus caught. For hours – nothing happened until Jesus got involved. And then the miracle came, pressed down, shaken together and running over. There is no scientific explanation for what occurred. The nets were the same. The water was the same. The boats were the same. The only thing that changed was Jesus got involved. And when Jesus gets involved, miracles happen as they did in the biblical days, now and forever.

In February of this year, I had an elective surgical procedure that was not covered by my health insurance. The surgery was an outpatient procedure and as expected, I was released and sent home that same day to recuperate. That evening when I stood up from my chair in the den, I nearly lost consciousness and fell to my knees. My wife and girls were there to catch me and helped me back into the chair. I thought nothing of it, attributing the lightheadedness to the anesthesia. I drank some water, had a light dinner and went to bed. During the night, I got up to go to the bathroom and the same thing happened again. My wife was there once again to catch me and help me back into the bed. The next day, the surgeon's office called to check on me and I reported these two episodes to them. He instructed me to come in immediately. My surgeon checked me out and immediately had me transported to the emergency room. I was tachycardic and had a pulse of 130. I received intravenous fluids and a battery of tests were performed. A normal hemoglobin (blood count) was 12 or 13. Mine was 9. I was admitted to the hospital to address the blood loss and anemia. The next day, my hemoglobin was down to 7, indicating worsening acute blood loss and anemia. I had another surgery in lieu of a transfusion. The day after the second surgery, my blood count was 10, and I was released the next day.

A few weeks after that ordeal, I received a letter from the insurance company stating that my claim for February 21st and 22nd was denied. It was denied because the treatment was the result of an elective surgery that was not covered by my insurance. The bill was $32,567.78. I was instructed to contact the hospital to work out a payment plan. What kind of payment plan would I have to have to cover close to $33k of unexpected expenses? I spoke with the insurance company several times, with my benefits director at work, and with my surgeon but got nowhere. Finally, I steadied myself long enough to read the rest of the letter. According to the insurance company, I could appeal the decision within 180 days of service. I sat and tried to write an appeal letter, but it was not flowing. I was later advised that I could request a peer-to-peer appeal, where my doctor could speak directly with the insurance company doctors to bring the situation to some type of resolve. The call was set-up and that's when I began praying. It was a long long shot. My surgeon even said, "it will take an act of God to get this reversed. The language of your coverage is crystal clear." That didn't scare me, in fact, it gave me hope. God specializes in miracles. God was now involved, and I was waiting for something miraculous to happen. An act of God was exactly what I was expecting.

On August 9th, I had a follow-up visit with my surgeon. When I walked in, the receptionist said, "Mr. Robertson, we were just talking about you. We received a fax from the insurance company just a few minutes ago. The denial was overturned. The insurance company is going to pay." The first words out of my mouth were thank you, Lord Jesus. My Thomas spirit rose up and I asked for the official documentation. I wanted to read it for myself. When I did, the very first line on the fax stated in all capital letters, DENIAL OVERTURNED ON 1ST APPEAL 8/8/2019. Was my prevail highly improbable? Yes. Are there natural or scientific laws to explain the overturning? No. Did the situation change when Jesus got involved? Yes. I experienced a miracle. I know for sure that God is still working miracles.

Simon said to Jesus, "... but because you say so," I will follow your instructions. Miracles happen not because of magic, or science, or coincidence. Miracles happen because Jesus commands them to happen. Do you really understand how powerful that is? Do you really understand what that means? It is the overwhelming difference between facts and truth. As mentioned several times throughout this book, facts are evidence-based. They are provable and easy to understand through our conscious phase of mind. In my miracle demonstration, the health plan language was clear. This hospitalization and treatment were not covered. It's a fact. I can point to it in the plan document (which I read of course). Truth is spiritual and principle-based. We discern the truth through the Christ mind. With facts, not a lot is possible above that which can be proved. In truth, all things are possible. When Jesus gets involved and speaks health, wealth, happiness, and success, miracles happen; people are healed, the hungry are fed, the poor become rich, the weak become strong, and insurance company denials are overturned even on the first appeal.

As spiritual beings who believe in the omniscience, omnipotence and omnipresence of God, we pay attention to facts, but our hope is built on nothing less than the truth that all things to our highest good are possible, plausible, and probable with God. It is impossible to build a prosperity consciousness solely on facts. It is the truth about God that shall make you free.

More on Facts vs. Truth

Let me tell you the story about Miss Charlene and Sister Vera. Ms. Charlene and Sister Vera have been friends since high school. Their mothers were best friends, and they spent a lot of time together. Miss Charlene went to church occasionally. She believed in God but would not consider herself as spiritual by any stretch of the imagination. Sister Vera, on the other hand, was an authentic and enthusiastic Christian. She still attends and serves in the church she grew up in and is a part of the evangelistic team. Both women have had struggles in their lives but have approached them differently. Miss Charlene believes more in dealing with the challenges of life through legal or letter-of-the-law means. Her approach is fact-based. Sister Vera takes everything to God, leaves it with Him and expects Him to work it out. Sister Vera uses a truth-based approach.

It was the end of the week and Miss Charlene was down in spirit. There was so much happening that she was overwhelmed and needed the comforting words of her Sister Vera. Miss Charlene has always liked being around Sister Vera because she was always positive and was the quintessential up-thinker. They met for dinner and dessert at their favorite restaurant Friday night after work. Miss Charlene began to talk all about her challenges. Sister Vera simply told her to focus on the truth, and she would be made free. Miss Charlene was somewhat disappointed. She expected pity and consoling. She expected enabling and commiserating prose, but no matter how much Miss Charlene described her situation, Sister Vera's answer was always the same. "… Come out from among them and be ye separated saith the Lord," (2 Corinthians 6:17 KJV) she'd say. She'd tell her to "pull out the truth from the facts and keep them separate. Focus on the truth and be set free."

Miss Charlene was growing annoyed. She felt that the woman she always depended on for guidance and encouragement was dismissing her with platitudes and Pollyanna. At one point in the conversation, she had worked herself up into what could only be described as the prelude to a nervous breakdown and wept. Sister Vera reached into her designer purse, retrieved some tissue and handed it to Miss Charlene. While Miss Charlene was regaining her composure, Sister Vera retrieved her bible, notepad and pen. She told Miss Charlene that if she knew the truth, she would be made free of her pain, misery, doubt, worry, sorrow and lack. Miss Charlene needed to build a consciousness of freedom. Using her bible and her wisdom, Sister Vera was going to help her. They spent the next hour working through Miss Charlene's issues to the truth. The diagram below illustrates their work.

Issue	Fact Consciousness Miss Charlene	The Truth What God Said	Conclusion Sister Vera
Health	You know I haven't been feeling well. I went to a specialist, and he said that there was no more that could be done. I just have to live with this condition for the rest of my life. In the end, it will probably kill me. Some days I feel good and some days I feel terrible. The fact is there is no cure. This is my lot in life.	"And suddenly, a woman who had a flow of blood for twelve years came from behind and touched the hem of His garment. For she said to herself, If only I may touch his garment, I shall be made well. But Jesus turned around, and when He saw her, He said, Be of good cheer daughter; your faith has made you well. And the woman was made well from that hour," (Matthew 9:20-22 NKJV). "Jesus Christ is the same yesterday, today, and forever," (Hebrews 13:8 NKJV).	The truth is that there is no such thing as an incurable life-long condition. Sickness is not your lot in life nor the will of God concerning you. Jesus is still healing. Know this truth. Tell the truth to come out from among those facts and be separated. Practice this truth and be made free.
Finances	You know our president changed the tax codes. I got a letter from the IRS stating that I owe $7,000. I've never had to pay and always received a refund. Where in the world am I going to find $7,000? The	"After Jesus and his disciples arrived in Capernaum, the collectors of the temple tax came to Peter and asked, doesn't your teacher pay the temple tax? Yes, He does, Peter replied. When Peter came into the house,	The truth is that because of your divinity and patrimony to God, you cannot be broke. There is not one obligation you will experience that God cannot provide. There is not one need you have that Jesus

Issue	Fact Consciousness Miss Charlene	The Truth What God Said	Conclusion Sister Vera
	fact is, I'm broke and don't have money to pay this bill and never will.	Jesus was the first to speak. What do you think Peter, he asked? From whom do the kings of the earth collect duty and taxes from their own children or from others? From others, Peter answered. Then the children are exempt, Jesus said to him. But so that we may not cause offense, go to the lake and throw out your line. Take the first fish you catch, open its mouth and you will find a four-drachma coin. Take it and give it to them for my taxes and yours," (Matthew 17:24-27 NIV).	cannot meet. There is not one bill you owe that God cannot pay. Expect your good from any and all sources, even ones that you don't know about. Know this truth. Tell the truth to come out from among those facts and be separated. Practice this truth and be made free.
Being Happy	I'm just not happy. There's so much going on. I really have nothing to be happy about. Maybe the Lord put this sadness on me to punish me for something I've done along the way. The devil is coming for me with this	"Happy are the people who are in such a state. Happy are the people whose God is the Lord," (Psalms 144:15 NKJV). "Delight yourself in the Lord, and He will give you the desires of your heart," (Psalms 37:4 NIV).	The truth is that there is no duality of power in the universe. The only power, the only presence is God, the good omnipotent: the everywhere present intelligent spirit of absolute good. Your God is Lord. Your Father is Lord. There is

Issue	Fact Consciousness Miss Charlene	The Truth What God Said	Conclusion Sister Vera
	constant sadness. The fact is, I don't have a thing to be happy about.		nothing to be sad about. There is nothing to fear. There is a place in you, a secret place, where everything is alright. That's where you go to commune with the Father. There is nothing but happiness, joy, and peace there. Go there. Know this truth. Tell the truth to come out from among those facts and be separated. Practice this truth and be made free.
The Job	My team at work just got word that because of a recent acquisition, some employees from the acquired company will be joining our team. My manager will need another supervisor and wants to promote someone from the current team. The fact is that I have the seniority and meet the qualifications except having a degree. I can't be promoted.	"I can do all things through Christ which strengthens me," (Philippians 4:13 KJV). "Ye are God, little children, and have overcome them because greater is He that is in you, than he that is in the world," (1 John 4:4 KJV).	The truth is that our Father is omniscient. He's all knowing. Through His omniscience, we are qualified to do anything we want to do. We know all we need to know through the Christ spirit within us. The Christ spirit is always there, giving instructions and ideas. You are more than qualified and worthy of that promotion. Know this truth. Tell

Issue	Fact Consciousness Miss Charlene	The Truth What God Said	Conclusion Sister Vera
			the truth to come out from among those facts and be separated. Practice this truth and be made free.

Sister Vera completed the last piece of the diagram and looked across the table at Miss Charlene. "Come on," she said. "What else you got?" Miss Charlene smiled and chuckled. She was finally getting the lesson. Every human being on the planet has a God-given right and expectation to live a life of good health, wealth, and happiness. We have a right to live a life of abundance and prosperity. As human beings, we engage in wrong-thinking and forget our true selves: we are divine. The bible was created to bring you the good news about yourself. I know for sure that God wants you to be prosperous even if requires a miracle.

Sister Vera could see not only a smile on Miss Charlene's face but hope and relief. There was a glowing presence about her. She was pushing away her "down-thinker" thoughts and excepting the truth. She had a glow of spiritual illumination and renewal. "I've got something else I want to tell you," Sister Vera said, flipping quickly through her bible in search of a scripture. "I want you to start acting as though you have already received what you're asking for. I need you to start digging some ditches."

"You want me to quit my job and dig ditches?" Miss Charlene asked. "What I look like digging ditches in high heels? God couldn't have shown you that."

"Naw girl," Sister Vera said. "Just listen to this story." Sister Vera began reading one of her favorite bible stories found in 2 Kings 3:9-18 NIV. "So the king of Israel set out with the king of Judah and the king of Edom. After a roundabout march of seven days, the army had no more water for themselves or for the animals with them. What! Exclaimed the king of Israel. Has the Lord called us three kings together only to deliver us into the hand of Moab? But Jehoshaphat asked, is there no prophet of the Lord here, through whom we may inquire of the Lord? An officer of the king of Israel answered, Elisha son of Shaphat is here. He used to pour water on the hands of Elijah [he was Elijah's personal servant]. Jehoshaphat said, the word of the Lord is in him. So the king of Israel and Jehoshaphat and the king of Edom went down to him. Elisha said to the king of Israel, why do you want to involve me? Go to the prophets of your father and the prophets of your mother. No, the king of Israel answered, because it was the Lord who called us three kings together to deliver us into the hands of Moab. Elisha said, as surely as the Lord Almighty lives, who I serve, if I did not have respect for the presence of Jehoshaphat king of Judah, I would not pay any attention to you. But now bring me a harpist. While the harpist was playing, the hand of the Lord came on Elisha, and he said thus saith the Lord, make this valley full of ditches. For thus saith the Lord, you will see neither wind, nor rain, yet this valley will be filled with water, and you, your cattle and your other animals will drink. This is an easy thing in the eyes of the Lord, he will also deliver Moah into your hands," (2 Kings 3:9-18 NIV).

"Moab was such a horrible ruler," Sister Vera began to explain. "It took three kings and their armies to even attempt to get him. And these kings under normal circumstances, shouldn't be working together. The scripture says that one king was an idolater, another would sell his soul for sex, and the other was walking outside the will of God for his people. They didn't feel as if they needed God. One king and army couldn't do it but surely three could. That's the mistake we make sometimes. We have a few wins, and we just forget all about God as the source of our supply. I liken the kings metaphysically to represent the channels of supply. We get so used to them and comfortable that we take our eyes off the source, which is God. We idolize our jobs, and our partners, and our long-term channels of good so much so that when they dry up, we lose our minds and give up hope. But our hope is not in the channel. Our hope is in the source, and because of His promises, everything we need and want to our highest good is already done."

"What do you mean metaphysically?" Miss Charlene asked in earnest.

"Metaphysical means beyond the physical," Miss Vera explained. "That's how I've learned to interpret the scriptures. I go beyond the literal meaning to pull out and understand what the words are saying to me. I believe this is why God refers to the scriptures as the living word. The word comes alive when we interpret it beyond the letter of the scripture and glean what it means to us."

"I get it," Miss Charlene said. "So for me, the prophet Elisha metaphysically represents the omniscience of God. I remember you persuading me to think of God as omnipresent, omniscient, and omnipotent (everywhere present, all knowing and intelligence, and all power). As a child of God, I am able to tap into that omniscience to get the understanding and knowledge I need to make the best decisions for my life, comfortable in knowing that I will be successful."

"That's right," Sister Vera said. "And digging the ditches means to act as if your good has already occurred. I use my vision board to carve out in my mind what it is that I want. I imagine myself living in it, riding in it, feeling good, energetic, and satisfied just as if I had it. I pray and listen to the leading of the Lord. I look and listen for signs and wonders. I look for people who have been sent to help me. I listen to their advice and counsel. So when the blessing and the good comes, like the water, there is a place for it in my world. I've dug a ditch or made a place for it in my experience. And I thank God and enjoy it, just like the kings, their armies, and their cattle enjoyed the once dry valley now full of water."

"What do you think the verse about seeing no wind and no rain means?" Miss Charlene asked.

"Well, for me, I think it means that sometimes our good, although it comes from God, it comes in ways that we don't expect," Miss Vera replied. "If you see storm clouds and you run outside and set a large pot in place, you're expecting the rain to fill the pot. If you are hot and you feel the wind, you are expecting to cool off. But sometimes our good comes to us in ways we don't even expect. The kings and their armies never expected to find water in the desert but that's how the Lord works sometimes."

"I'm picking up on another lesson," Miss Charlene said. Sister Vera was excited to hear. "I think that God delivers His good to us in unexpected ways because He wants us to focus on Him, the source and not the channel. Once you set in your mind that the only way something can come to you is through the way it has always come, you've gotten too channel-focused and less God-focused. My daddy used to sing a song in church that said, the Lord, will provide. Some way or another, the Lord will provide."

Sister Vera and Miss Charlene had a great time talking about the awesomeness of God and metaphysically interpreting the story that Sister Vera introduced. They discussed why Elisha had such disdain for two of the kings, and the purpose of the harpist Elisha requested. They both left the restaurant singing and rejoicing, knowing that God the good was going to move in Miss Charlene's life and move in a marvelous way.

Think on These Things

1. What is the working definition of prosperity from the reading?
2. Why do you think the principle of prosperity was frowned upon or dismissed in the early days of the church?
3. Why are thoughts of jealousy and envy out of order and place in a prosperity consciousness?
4. What's the difference between the facts and the truth?
5. What is the definition of a miracle?
6. What does the term "metaphysical" mean?
7. Metaphysically, describe the relationship between Miss Charlene and Sister Vera?
8. From the 2 Kings scripture, why do you think Elisha asked for music before revealing the prophesy?

CONCLUSION

Arise and Walk

"After this there was a feast of the Jews, and Jesus went up to Jerusalem. Now there is in Jerusalem by the Sheep Gate a pool, which is called in Hebrew, Bethesda, having five porches. In these lay a great multitude of sick people, blind, lame, paralyzed, waiting for the moving of the water. For an angel went down at a certain time into the pool and stirred up the water; then whoever stepped in first, after the stirring of the water, was made well of whatever disease he had. Now a certain man was there who had an infirmity thirty-eight years. When Jesus saw him lying there, and knew that he already had been in that condition a long time, He said to him, do you want to be made well? The sick man answered Him, sir, I have no man to put me into the pool when the water is stirred up; but while I am coming, another steps down before me. Jesus said to him, rise, take up your bed and walk. And immediately the man was made well, took up his bed, and walked," (John 5:1-9 NKJV).

I can't imagine the levels of agony and misery this man endured. The scripture does not disclose the man's age but for 38 years of his life, he had been ill and unable to get to his healing. He knew where to go, what to do, and was sure that the outcome would be successful as he had seen others who were healed. I can imagine that day after day, night after night, as he laid there on his mat, feeling a sense of overwhelming defeat yet planning and strategizing on how to get to his healing. As if his physical pain was not enough, he was in a perpetual mental state of disappointment, defeat, and sorrow. And he just wanted what everyone else had – a life that was upright, active and mobile. But for 38 years, he suffered day after day.

At the beginning of this book, I told you the story of how David, a little boy and untrained fighter, defeated the Philistine Goliath with a smooth stone and a sling shot. I began the book with that story to convey a lesson of triumph, of hope, and of victory. That story served as the cornerstone of this work because the message I wanted to convey as you read through these chapters is that with God, all things are possible. No matter the odds, no matter the ridicule and opinions of others, no matter what your mother's story was or your father's story, there is hope and victory in our Father, Teacher and Wayshower, God. David had zeal, faith, determination, and a weapon and God made him a conqueror and hero. The man at Bethesda had nothing: no zeal, no faith, no determination, and no weapon and Jesus healed him. Whatever you have, wherever you are, whatever your condition, you can defeat it with the presence of the omnipresent, omniscient, and omnipotent spirit of God, which is the motor masterfully placed inside of you. You don't have to succumb to the threats of the bully or the defeat of seeing others prosper while you sit stagnant in place or on your bed. You can be healed. You can return to an upright state. It's already done.

In this book, I shared my thoughts on what I know for sure about God. I've never written a book before. It was not easy, but it was my assignment for this time. I hope that there was one story, one scripture, one lesson herein that made you think; made you reexamine your walk; and most of all, called you to action. God is a God of command and action: let there be; go, and sin no more; stretch out thy hand; drop your nets on the right side; come out from among them; roll the stone aside; Lazarus, come out; rise, take up your bed and walk. Even the man at pool living in agony had to act – he had to answer the Lord's question: do you want to be made well?

That's the question I pose to you: do you want to be healed? Do you want to live a happy, healthy, and prosperous life? Do you want all the things that money can buy and all the things it can't? Then you must rise-up in consciousness, take-up your bed (all the old teachings and empty beliefs about who you are and who God is) and walk. You must walk into your divinity, your inheritance, and all the powers you have inside you that make you a powerhouse. You must do as the prodigal son did and come to yourself – as the masterfully made child of God. A mind-renewing exercise must be performed. Your healing, miracle, or breakthrough is not dependent upon anyone! Nothing and no one is required to pull you up and place you in your good, which was surely the hope of the man at Bethesda. If you want to be healed, if you want a new life, if you want to experience the promises of God, you must seek God and build a relationship with Him. You must take up your bed and walk; walk into the abundant and fulfilling life you were meant to live.

I have just one more story to tell you. It's about a woman I now know God wanted me to meet for the purpose of this assignment. Her name is Paula. We met in a creative writing course I took a few years ago. This was when I thought I was going to be a famous and prolific romance novelist. Each week, our instructor taught techniques and skills to help potential writers master their craft. For each class, we had to produce a two to three-page paper written in our respective genre and relative to the instruction the prior week. Each week, we read our work aloud in class and gleaned feedback from our classmates. Paula was a very good writer, much stronger than me. I looked forward to hearing the surprise ending of one of her "who done it" mystery pieces.

At the end of this particular class, the instructor lectured on memoir writing. The assignment for next week was to produce the first two to three pages of our life's story. Each student would read their work during class. The instructor then introduced us to the benefits and importance of peer editing. We were responsible for getting our work to our editing partner for critique before the next class. Critiques would also be read aloud in class. Paula was my editing partner.

I really can't remember exactly what I wrote about. I think it was about the day I realized that I was a real human being. On the Saturday before class, as we agreed, Paula and I exchanged our papers via email. Hers was entitled The Great Mystery, which was intriguing. I couldn't wait to read it. In her email, she apologized for the few extra pages and said she was looking forward to my honest critique. My mouth was agape for the entire read. The first sentence read, "I should be dead." We learned in class to grip the reader's attention with the first sentence. It worked, and in the next eight pages, she justified her opening statement:

- Both her parents argued incessantly before finally divorcing when she was in sixth grade;
- She was mistreated (now referred to as bullying) the first five years of grammar school because she was uber smart;
- She was suspended in her junior year of high school for fighting and bullying; also the year she officially became a "mean girl."
- After high school, she was accepted at the schools of her choice, but her parents could not agree on how they would share the cost and ended up not paying at all. She went to a state school, worked full-time, and paid for it herself.
- She was promiscuous in college (she used another three-letter word), which was the reason (she believes) she was raped by her boyfriend in her senior year of college;
- She was fired from her first three jobs out of college for being insubordinate and difficult to work with;
- She married the love of her life who later left her because after several failed attempts, she could not conceive;
- She never really forgave her parents for not supporting her throughout college and had an estranged relationship with them both especially after they both remarried;
- Realizing she had trouble working for someone, she started her own management consulting business, but it failed in the first year;
- At age 38, she was diagnosed with breast cancer; she beat it but was out of work for a year and lost her job and her home;
- She found a job she liked but was laid-off after three years;

- She left her church home after the new pastor was angry and lost his temper in front of the congregation over parishioners disrespecting him by parking in his reserved space; and
- At 45, she was diagnosed with manic depression, which she treated with alcohol, marijuana, and promiscuity.

In her narrative, she spoke about being so paralyzed from depression, she could barely function. She said she kept thinking about her life and all that she had been through and was just in a downward cycle of doom and gloom. Some days, she just couldn't get out of bed and when she did, it was to get some weed or a drink so she could try to work two or three days of the five-day work week. She saw death as an emergency exit. She knew the day would come where she couldn't take it anymore and would have to exit. It was just a matter of time. But something happened.

Her one friend managed to convince her to come to church with her. She had not been to church since the "man of God" went off on the congregation at her old church. But this one Sunday, she decided to go. It was the *Monument of Faith Evangelistic Church*, pastored by the late Apostle Richard D. Henton. It was your typical charismatic Pentecostal church with loud singing, shouting, speaking in tongues and rip-roaring preaching. But when all that calmed down, her miracle happened. Apostle Henton had an altar call. People who were sick or had problems could come to the altar for prayer. Paula's friend went to the alter but Paula stayed in her seat. Right before Apostle Henton prayed, he called her out. "There is a woman sitting in her seat who knows she should be up here. You've had a rough time but drinking and smoking [marijuana] is not the answer. Christ is the answer. Get up and come down here whoever you are."

Paula said before she knew it, she was at the altar in front of Apostle Henton. He asked her, "do you want to be delivered?" to which she said yes. He laid his hands on her and prayed for her. She wrote about an "overwhelming heat" that suddenly came over her body before she spiraled to the floor. She said when she came to herself, she was in the car with her friend, crying tears of joy, relief, and freedom. I can't remember all the details of her paper but somewhere she repeated, "I should be dead, but God saved my life."

I remember telling her that she should definitely write her memoirs. It could be such a help and inspiration to people, especially those hurting maybe in greater ways than she experienced. I also told her about my idea for this book to which she also encouraged me for the same reasons.

So what are these stones? These stones are the firm truths about God and ourselves we know for sure. We use them as tools to learn, advance, and cultivate the happiness, health, and prosperity we are to experience as children of God. Like David, we use these stones as weapons, against the giant challenges, threats and illusions of lack, sickness, and distress whether imposed by others or self. These stones are also reminders of the challenges and lessons we've learned through our experiences. We lay these stones down and walk on them on this road called life. They can be heavy so like my friend, Paula, we lay them down and use them as steppingstones to our divinity and every desire of our hearts.

I so badly wanted to name these stones for you as faith, love, prosperity, wisdom, and so on, but I couldn't. Like David, you must deal with these tools, weapons, and lessons according to your personal experience and where you are in consciousness and awareness. I cannot prescribe them for you. That, I believe, is one of the beauties of true salvation and a relationship with God. It's personal – just between you and the Father.

Whether you gather five, eight, or ten stones, the call is the same. It's time to arise, take up your bed and walk! The purpose of this book was to move you to action. It is not necessary to sit and wait for days, months, or years at Bethesda. Your transformation is at hand. You have all the power you need inside of you. It's time to ARISE AND WALK!

EPILOGUE

*"All humanity's problems stem from man's
inability to sit quietly in a room alone."*

Blaise Pascal

You have finished the book! Congratulations and thank you. My PRAYER is that YOU ARE THE ONE! My prayer throughout this project was to share a scripture, lesson, story, or pose a question that would touch, stir, or propel just one person to positive action. Everyone who reads it out of support for me or out of pure curiosity, will not like it and that's okay. I'm looking for one person who is encouraged to take on a more active role in their spiritual development. I hope YOU ARE THE ONE. I encourage you to spend some time with your mind that you may live a happy, healthy, and wealthy life.

And so it is!

RESOURCES

Cady, Emillie. *Complete Premium Collection: Lessons In Truth; How I Used Truth; God a Present Help.* Delaware: McAllister Editions, 2015. Print.

Cambridge Dictionary, "miracle," accessed September 26, 2019 Dictionary. cambridge.org/dictionary/miracle.

Fillmore, Charles. *The Twelve Powers.* Unity Village, MO: 1930. Print.

Lexico-Oxford Dictionary, "Karma," accessed September 26, 2019, Lexico. com/dictionary/Karma.

Lexico-Oxford Dictionary, "lexicon," accessed September 26, 2019, Lexico.com/dictionary/Karma.

MarTella-Whitsett, Linda. *Divine Audacity.* Virginia: Hampton Roads, 2015. Print.

Merriam-Webster Dictionary, "anxiety," accessed September 26, 2019, Merriam-Webster.com/dictionary/anxiety.

Merriam-Webster Dictionary, "wicked," accessed September 26, 2019, Merriam-Webster.com/dictionary/wicked.

"Not a Repeat, But a Rekindling of Hope: Chronicles: Not Just a Repeat." The BibleProject.com. Web. August 2017.

"Your Key to Love, Good Health, Prosperity, and Successful Living." ScienceofLivingOnline.com. Web. 2019.

Warch, William. *The New Thought Christian*. California: DeVorss & Company, 1977. Print. Spiritual Communion Service – author unknown.